Lessons in Surviving Suicide
A Letter to my Daughter

Lessons in Surviving Suicide
A Letter to my Daughter

Vonne Solís

gatekeeper press™

Columbus, Ohio

Lessons in Surviving Suicide: A Letter to My Daughter

Published by Gatekeeper Press
2167 Stringtown Rd, Suite 109
Columbus, OH 43123-2989
www.GatekeeperPress.com

Jacket design © Vonne Solís

Library of Congress Control Number: 2020946835

ISBN: 9781662904998
eISBN: 9781662905001

For my family, with love

Books by Vonne Solís

Divine Healing – Transforming Pain into Personal Power, A Guide to Heal Pain from Child Loss, Suicide and Other Grief

The Power of Change – A Path to Enlightenment

Contents

Introduction 1

Regret 3

Loving You 9

Dreams 12

Failure 16

Forgiveness 22

Hope 26

Acceptance 30

Envy 34

Willingness 38

Longing 42

Choice 45

Pain 49

Suffering 56

Anger 61

Trust 67

Self-Love 72

Joy 77

Ambition 82

Identity 87

Limitations 93

Change 100

Trauma and Post-Traumatic Stress Disorder 106

Gratitude 116

Perseverance 122

Isolation 127

Support 133

Desire 140

Suicide & Stigma 145

Survival 158

Vulnerability 167

Disappointment 172

Shame 178

Fear 186

Compassion 191

Courage 198

Confusion 203

Faith 208

Abandonment 213

Peace 218

Relief 224

Intention 231

Self-Worth 239

Strength 244

Completion 251

Resources 264

About the Author 266

Introduction

When I first became bereaved in 2005, after the suicide of my daughter Janaya at the age of twenty-two, more than anything I wanted another bereaved parent to tell me exactly what I could expect from my grief. What would it be like? Would it ever end? What would happen to my family? Critically, how could I go on living without my child? I was terrified. I had thousands of questions and no real answers. The future looked bleak.

Fifteen years later, I am that parent I so desperately wanted to learn from in the beginning of my bereavement. One of my greatest struggles in my grief has come from not knowing why my daughter chose to die. I still don't know. The fact that there can never be any closure for this part of my loss experience has complicated my grief and trapped me in the numerous ways that I explore throughout this book.

When I was diagnosed with Post-Traumatic Stress Disorder in 2014, I knew that to have any hope of fully healing from my daughter's suicide, despite the progress I had made, I would have to drill down and explore the issues impeding my full recovery that went back to my very first days as a newly bereaved parent. I felt there was no better way to revisit this emotional pain than by writing my daughter directly, to ensure my thoughts and words could flow unfiltered.

With the exception of some light editing, this is a raw and candid sharing of my innermost struggles as a bereaved mom, to help newly bereaved parents who have lost their child to suicide, navigate early grief and avoid some of the common pitfalls. The body of each chapter has been written as a letter to my daughter. The recounting of my struggles here and the lessons learned at the end of each chapter are the result of introspection looking back that only time can give us.

While all bereaved parents have thousands of questions related to the death of their child, the suicide of our child presents its own unique questions and challenges. While the answers we seek are as personal to every bereaved parent as their path is through grief, it is my hope that everyone reading this book will find information to help them on their journey from all that I've learned looking back on my own.

Child loss is horrendous. Though much of what I've written to my daughter is heart wrenching, I've found it is only by boldly peeling away the layers of pain to discover what is really lurking beneath, that I could ever hope to find myself again after losing her to suicide. I'm certain the same is true for every parent who has lost their child, too.

Time is bittersweet for all bereaved parents. The more it passes, the more we can feel challenged to accept the finality of losing our child. Yet, I remain optimistic that we can heal from the pain. To what degree this is remains questionable, given the struggles countless bereaved parents face to find healing, even years later.

In the end, I wonder. Does it come down to the choice we make about how we want to live? What we want to let go of and actually can? What we want for our future? Or, is there so much more to consider?

Regret

My dearest daughter, if I knew then what I know now, my world would be a different place. At least, that's what I tell myself. I would be living with fewer regrets. You'd still be here. Life would be beautiful. In contrast, and what tears my inner world apart, is the thought that perhaps more knowledge wouldn't have changed the outcome of your ending. That I am simply choosing to believe I could have saved your life, if only I had known and done things differently. No matter how insightful or more helpful I could or should have been, you'd still be gone. And so, I struggle.

I've begun to ask myself, years after your death, whose story have I been living? Yours or mine? My inner struggle wanting and needing to let you go, contrasted sharply with clinging to you with all I have left; which is my pain, intertwine incessantly throughout my days. I imagine you as you might be today. What you'd look like. What you'd be doing. Would you be married? Would you be a mom? Would you be happy? Photographs *always* stop your story at the same place and time. How I've wanted them to change and age you.

You are gone and I am here. It seems nearly impossible for me to find the peace I know *could* be mine if I could just accept your death, but I can't. Is this mother's longing for her child destined to haunt me until my own demise?

From the moment I learned of your choice to leave this planet, I respected it. I didn't agree with it, but never once did I make you wrong for choosing to leave a life of pain that only with your passing, did I understand. I was blind and deaf to your cries for help, feeble as they may have seemed. I wanted for you what all good parents want for their child. A decent life filled with wonderful opportunities that matched your brilliance. I only saw the brilliance. Anything else I dismissed as minor concerns that all parents feel watching their child grow into adulthood. I wasn't sure whether to hang on tight to you or let you go.

I wasn't sure how far you could fly on your own little one, until one day, I became brave enough to test the waters. I discovered too late your wings were broken. Looking back, I think you already knew this. With no small amount of irony, I realize now, you already knew way more than I gave you credit for. Fragile yet fierce: that's how I think of you. I wonder: did you contemplate before your death the failures of the one person you should have been able to trust the most with all of your challenges? Not being able to find the support you needed, does this make me a terribly inadequate mother? Or, am I just human after all, and it is my own arrogance that keeps me tied to the belief I could have saved you? That I should have saved you?

The choice that is mine to relish the days I have left, soaking up the endless beauty all this earth offers the living, leaves me blank. I don't feel joy or excitement the way many people do and even take for granted. I can't find meaning in anything I once could. My regrets are many. That I can't turn back the clock for even just a second to have said or done something different to help you. That I should have prayed for wisdom sooner. That I didn't get to know you better. I feel I missed out.

How useful it is to ponder regret is debatable. That the word's very meaning is tied to disappointment, sorrow and loss, how could I, in my grief, not hold onto regret? How could I let any of my regrets go? How could I ever *not* feel disappointment and sorrow that you died? Worse yet that you chose to take your life?

I am filled with regret when I think of the thoughts that must have been swirling through your mind as you struggled with your choice to live or die. And if you didn't struggle, what does that say about me? Your mom who was supposed to guide you and who loved you more than life itself? Or about your family who also loved you dearly? Clearly, mistakes must have been made. With no note left behind, you've left all of us guessing.

I never want to make you wrong for what you did, which has left me in this state that cannot wholly be defined. Sometimes it feels like indifference. Sometimes it feels like frustration, anger and impatience. Sometimes, it feels as though I am totally incapable of loving again, but this I know is just the safeguard I put up to protect me in my vulnerability. Often, the state I'm in is one of sadness. Always, it is one of pain.

I know that as my child, you did not intend to subject me to what feels like a life sentence of suffering. You probably never even thought about the consequences of your actions. If you did, likely you miscalculated the turmoil that would (and did) result in the wake of your death. In fact, I think you'd be quite surprised to see how much you were and still are loved. I believe you chose death partly because you did not understand this love. Certainly not mine. But there I go again, shifting the basis of your choice to die to me, when in fact, maybe I had nothing to do with it at all. This is one of the great paradoxes I struggle with daily.

I admit, my ignorance of depression and my inability to help you more than I did when you were alive has caused me to regret many choices I made at various times throughout your young life. Thinking about all the *"what ifs"* has been emotionally crippling. I've beat myself up more than what is good or fair, but frankly, what else am I to do with all this pain? To surrender it would mean I must re-think my beliefs and somehow restructure them. I know, that sounds a lot like therapy talk and it is. But tell me, how am I, and as your mom, having failed at the most important role on this planet, which was to safeguard and care for you, to do this? That would mean letting it be okay that I am still here, and you are not. That in accepting my failures, I could also accept I did the best I could with what I knew at the time.

It's one thing to intellectually understand this complexity, but a whole different matter to shift my beliefs, especially where they concern your death. So far, no one has been able to help me with this. I know. I must help myself. Believe me, I am trying. But, the other twist to this enormous challenge is that I find it almost too painful to revisit the memories and feelings I still have from the second I learned you were gone. They are as vivid in my mind as if your passing happened just yesterday.

What I regret the most is that while I may not have been able to change the outcome of your death, I would have paid serious attention to the warning signals telling me that something wasn't right. Looking back, I can see the signs were all there. I just didn't know what they were or what to do with them. Today I do. I would have listened to you more. Hugged you tighter. I would have called you on your thoughts. And even though you may not have been honest with me, I would have done all I could within my power to make you feel safe, secure and loved through whatever was troubling you. I would have told you how afraid I was for you. That I feared some type of harm would come to you that was out of my control. I would have dared you to prove me wrong.

Given all this is hypothetical and I *can't* ever change the outcome of your dying, I would certainly be kinder to myself a lot sooner in my grief, by accepting my limitations as a human being. Years of suffering where I denied myself the self-love, self-compassion

and kindness I deserve has not proven helpful to my
because this is a story unfolding, I can promise you that ı ..
working on loving myself. On forgiving myself. On feeling grateful
that you were in my life for the time you were.

Knowing your ending isn't making any of this easy. However,
I can say that little by little, as I become more trusting of myself
and consider the impact this enormous loss of you has had on me,
the edges of my heart are softening. I am seeing things with greater
clarity. I realize that treating myself with kindness and gentleness
will go a long way to easing some of my despair. It may not bring
you back, but it will help me live again.

If I knew then what I know now, I would tell newly bereaved
parents that regret is inevitable for any parent who loses their child.
For those who lose their child to suicide, there will be many regrets.
Self-blame will likely top the list as parents try to make sense of
where they went wrong. The signs they missed that resulted in
their child's death. How they could be so stupid. So blind. So
thoughtless. So careless. So self-absorbed. So misinformed. So
powerless to help.

I would tell them that wasting years thinking about regret is
pointless and not at all conducive to their healing. However, most
parents won't be able to avoid feeling regret for all they did or didn't
do and blaming themselves for their child's death. It's natural to
beat themselves up over and over again, because regret is at the
center of much of their pain and anger. Only time will carry them
to that place where one day, they feel ready to consider whether
they want to live with more joy or suffering. Understanding that
staying embroiled in regret for all they did or didn't do will only
serve to negatively impact their healing process.

I would also remind those new to grief that while it is inevitable many bereaved parents may end up living with a combination of suffering and joy, it may be helpful to consider that giving up regret for their child, rather than themselves may be easier to do. Any bereaved parent that would choose to live their life defined only by their agony (myself included) robs their child of the chance to be honored for who they were and the life they did live.

Loving You

What can I possibly say about loving you sweet child? Except that I didn't know how much I did until you were gone. I knew I loved you as my living child. Every parent feels that glorious moment of change the instant their child is born. Losing you was much the same. After your death, a profound feeling of a deeper, all-encompassing and unconditional love for you and others emerged from my soul. In loving you as my lost child, I've had to divide this love in two: loving you in memory of all that we had together and loving you as spirit. It gets complicated.

Ask any parent to imagine their child as spirit. Imagine what their answer would be. Well, that's how I feel. I struggle with releasing you to what I imagine must be some type of energy form in some type of other world. Sometimes I imagine this as color. Sometimes as waves of energy. Other times I imagine you would appear as pure white light.

When I do imagine you as infinite spirit, yet as a being that can still embody the physical traits you had on earth as my child, I struggle, feeling that's an unfair representation of who you really are now. I also wonder why I would ever expect you to hang onto this one painful lifetime. I know you have become so much more in death. When is it appropriate for me to let you go as my child? To set you free from the grief that ties me to my longing for you.

What worries me most is that I'll never see you again. I feel incredible disappointment and sadness when I think about this. I tell myself that my spiritual beliefs should outweigh those I have as a mom living with a broken heart. I have to believe that somehow, someday, we will meet again and recognize each other instantly. If not in physical form, then surely in spirit? In whatever way this may happen, I know it can never again be as we were. It saddens me deeply that we won't get another chance.

I am also saddened by the collateral damage as a result of the grief I feel from losing you that has consumed me. It has diminished the love I'm able to feel for everyone else, except your brother of course. I can't seem to get my heart working again the way I want it to. I've spent years trying to feel something more than just pain. I feel great disappointment that my living loved ones are missing out on me. Still, they stick around, even though I often feel it's just you and me kid.

If I knew then what I know now, I would tell newly bereaved parents not to ever question the love they felt for their lost child. It will have been enough. After years of thinking about my child's choice to die, I am certain it is not because she thought we didn't love her enough. Love did not factor into her decision to end her life. I would remind other bereaved parents it is likely the same for them.

It is vital that parents whose child has chosen to die by suicide trust that their child knew they loved them and felt supported by them in every way possible. Sometimes, just reminding themselves of this has to be enough for grieving parents. They can and will torture themselves endlessly if they believe their love for their child was not enough to keep that child living. And while every child's death by suicide makes it difficult for any parent to believe their love wasn't enough to keep their child living, sometimes, trusting that they did do their best to make sure their child knew the depth of their love is all they will have to keep going.

Together as bereaved parents and wherever our deceased children are now, we must believe with all our heart that our children did know how much we loved them, and that we will continue loving them until our last breath.

Dreams

W hat dreams I had for you, darling girl. For me. For our family. Giving them up has been hard. Pointless even, if I've had nothing to replace them with. From the moment you were born, I had dreams for you. As you grew, my dreams did too. I only wish you'd had some yourself.

After you died, I found your poetry and other writing that clearly showed how angry you were. Your mood was dark, morbid and completely opposite to all the wonderful things we talked about. I asked myself time and time again after you died, who were you? Why did you never, not once, come to me in your pain?

While your thoughts may have been the ramblings of a young person trying to find her way in the world, I was completely unaware of this darker side of you. I only saw your brilliance and the opportunities available from the choices put before you. Not once did I think these weren't enough.

I dreamed you could become anything you wanted to be and told you so. Many times. I thought that surely, when others saw your talent and gave you encouragement, you understood this. When you continually quit things and showed little motivation, I struggled to understand why a good and stable life and all that this entailed was not enough. Until I felt your pain.

I realize now that some people are not capable of dreaming. As my child, I wish I'd known how to help you dream. How to help you want dreams for your life.

I also wish I'd known that you couldn't really be on your own. I fear our chatter over endless cups of tea talking about my hopes for your future was all for nothing. That my words were just words. Sometimes I think back to how stupid I must have looked to you.

It must seem selfish of me to make the pain I feel today as important as yours. I never would have done this when you were living. Looking back, never in a million years would I have pressed you to be more than who you were capable of being. I would have tossed every dream I had for you in a second to help you shape just one of your own. And, if you still had none, what I wouldn't give to just sit and hold you now.

Often, I have contemplated my life as it may have been with you still in it. I imagine our mother and daughter outings. Going shopping. You still telling me what to wear. We'd still have serious talks, but I would make sure we had more fun and adventure. I wouldn't care about the status quo or push you to make choices based on what I thought was best for you. I would dream less and listen more. I would respect your decision to live the way you felt most at ease. I would be more flexible in my thinking. Most importantly, I would open my eyes.

I didn't see then what I should have seen because I didn't want to. My dreams were made of hallmark stuff. Not in a fantasy sort of way, but one where I truly believed that what I wanted for you was entirely possible and would ensure you got the most out of life. My love for you and the rest of the family was a big deal to me. My dreams reflected this. What a wake-up call I had when you up and suddenly died.

As a result of your death, I don't really dream anymore. I'm not sure if this is a good or bad thing. Do we need to have dreams to live a meaningful life? When I do experience brief and unexpected moments of reverie, they just as quickly slip away. I am reminded of my limitations, where I simply do not have the capacity to dream like I did before.

If I did have a last remaining one though, it would of course be that you never died. But, because this is not possible, I have to dream instead that you are safe and at peace, wherever you are, and that you will always stay near to me.

If I knew then what I know now, I would tell newly bereaved parents that as time goes on, they can expect to be crushed by unfulfilled dreams they had for their lost child. It took me years to accept that the dreams I had for my daughter and our family of four instantly vanished with her suicide. I felt nothing but sadness that the dreams of my surviving loved ones had been crushed just as fast, too. Since then, I've found it exceedingly difficult to come up with new dreams for me and our little family of three.

It is important for newly bereaved parents to remember that surviving children may also have dreams that included their brother or sister who died, or one that would have made their sibling proud. It is essential they talk to their living children about their lost dreams and feelings, and help them come up with a revised dream, over time.

While many bereaved parents must go on for the sake of their surviving children, it is natural to feel less of a parent and more of a sad, scrap of a human being after losing a child. Parents may no longer have the energy to love and care for their partners and even their children in the same way they did. Because of the grief parents are expressing, it is common for surviving children to think they should have died instead. My son said this to me more than once. It is important to trust that one day, they will feel stronger and once again be able to dream for the child or children they do have left. This is especially important to remember for parents who feel guilty about being absent for any length of time.

I believe that part of the problem bereaved parents may have not being able to dream again may lie in the fact that it's hard to see a future without their child in it. For parents who have lost their only child, I do not pretend to know what their grief is like. There will be different challenges for them than for parents who do have surviving children. For those lucky enough to still have a child or children living, they may worry as I did, that they are robbing them of much of the happiness they deserve by the very nature of their bereavement. As a grown man fifteen years after the death of his sister, my son has assured me this is not the case.

These days, I am choosing to focus on how lucky I am to have my son and how lucky he is to have doting parents who love him more than life itself. Exactly the same as we did before. I know he feels the same way. We are very close. As parents, we have made every effort through the years to ensure our son has never been forgotten in his grief or that he feels left out as we've trudged our way forward in our own. We often talk about his sister.

It is good for bereaved parents to remember that while it's true that families can never be put back together in the same way they existed before the loss of a child, we do go on to exist. Time is the one thing that grief can never stop. These days, it is my son who is teaching me to dream again.

Failure

M y dearest daughter, I feel like an abysmal failure
sometimes. I spent years after you died trying to prove
to myself and others how strong I was. How capable
I was, despite how broken I really felt. I didn't even realize that's
what I was doing. Like other bereaved parents, I threw myself into
a good cause to honor you. People suggested it was cathartic. It
wasn't. I eventually learned this was more self-punishment than
anything else.

It's somewhat easy on one level going out into the world,
putting on the mask you want others to see. But I found the world
demands much from those in pain. Eventually, it becomes difficult
to keep up the charade.

While I have accomplished more than I thought I could, and
maybe even some things that others would be content to have, I have
yet to feel successful. My feelings related to success are overshadowed
by what I fear is my biggest failure of all: *that I didn't save you. Why
could I not save you?* This is the one question I find myself continually
grappling with. I fear that no number of books I read or amount of
therapy I undergo is likely to give me a satisfactory answer.

It makes sense to me that a parent who has lost their child in
any manner would feel haunted by this question. But, the sense of
failure one may have because they couldn't save their child who
died by natural causes, or in an accident, may feel different than
for those whose child *chose* to no longer live. What bigger failure

could there be for a parent? There is no logic that seems sufficient to explain any suicide, but especially not the suicide of a young person.

The list of things I fear I did to fail you is long. What I may have done to help you is less clear. I haven't reached the point where I can focus only on the good memories and just be grateful you were in my life. Which brings me to another question that has continually challenged me. If I could do it all again and if it had to be exactly the same way, would I, knowing how it ended? Several bereaved parents I met right after your death told me without skipping a beat that they would. None of their children had died by suicide. I felt horrible for not being so sure.

Today, I know I have a choice whether or not I want to put the feeling of this enormous failure behind me. The one where I didn't save you. I want so much and without hesitation to yell to the world that I would do anything to have and raise you one more time, even if I had to do it in the same way with the same outcome. But this means I would have to accept my inadequacies that led to my failures and your death. Not to mention the almost certain lifetime of pain that I am now living. Which is where I'm stuck. I can likely over time, learn to forgive myself my failings as a parent in general, but I am having difficulty accepting any failure on my part that may have contributed to your wanting to die. *Why did you want to die?*

There is a part of me that understands as humans, we all have failures. Every other one I have dealt with in my life and moved on from. How I may have failed you as a mom in *any* way, not just that I was too blind to see the help you needed, has been almost too much for me to bear. This inner struggle of not knowing to what degree my ineptness may have contributed to your suicide, and because it's clear you didn't trust me with your pain, has left me struggling with what once was agonizing, is now a particularly difficult type of grief.

Not understanding your pain back then, I feel I now must bear the weight of responsibility for your suicide, sweet girl. It's easy to see with hindsight that had I known the seriousness of your mental health I would have searched endlessly to get you the help you needed. I would have accepted that your life was going to look different from the one I had dreamed of for you. I would have told you about the concern I felt somewhere deep within me that you could die one day, and I DID NOT want that to happen.

I would have insisted you be honest with me to help me understand what you were feeling. I would have told you over and over I would have done anything to make you feel safe and secure. That we could work through the challenges together, step by step, even if this meant you lived at home forever. I would have been happy being the one who always made the tea.

If I knew then what I know now, I would tell newly bereaved parents whose child has died by suicide that it will always be tempting for them to look back and incessantly berate themselves for all they should have done differently. In the end, they will come to realize that focusing only on their failures is nothing but another form of self-torture.

In my situation, I found that without the blinders on (they came off as soon as I learned of my daughter's suicide), it was easy to see I'd had a child in need who was different from what I expected her to be. She was likely too vulnerable and uncertain of what she was feeling to ask for help back then. She probably didn't even know who to ask. We weren't having the same discussions on mental health that we are today.

In looking back, I also realized I never talked to my daughter about her emotional pain. Even though I suspected something wasn't quite right by some of the behavior she was displaying as a teen (social isolation, anger, lack of motivation), it was too frightening for me to imagine anything may be seriously wrong. I put the moodiness and her sometimes antagonistic behavior down to the uncertainty and confusion many young people face growing into adulthood.

By the time she turned twenty-two in early February, my daughter had quit university only a few months into her courses. She was displaying a general disinterest with life and having trouble holding a job. I was worried, but still didn't get it. Not even a couple of months later when she started making amends in her life. I remember being surprised when she told me she had contacted an old boyfriend to apologize for any hurt she may have caused him. I was delighted when she called me one day to tell me what a great mom I was. I was especially pleased, though surprised, when she insisted on taking a swim in our pool on a cold day in early July when she hated to swim. She died a couple of weeks later.

Despite changes in her behavior, I didn't understand the serious trouble my child was in. I just thought she was facing the usual struggles growing up. Had I known more about suicide and been able to detect the signs that today I understand as a warning of the risk of suicide, I would have been more persistent in getting her the help she needed. I would not have let her out of my sight.

Having struggled with depression throughout my bereavement, today I also understand the limitations my child faced in helping herself. To probably even care about getting help. I know for a fact (regardless of all that I write here) that loved ones do not factor in the choice one may be contemplating about whether they want to live or die.

Having said this, knowing all of what I do know now certainly would have helped me be a better support to my daughter. Maybe it even would have kept her alive. For example, I would never have expected her to do anything she felt incapable of doing (such as staying in university, working, living on her own). I would have repeatedly asked her about her intentions to die by suicide, no matter how improbable or silly a notion this may have seemed. I would have held her hand more. Sat with her in silence. Hugged her tighter.

The fact that too late and only after she was gone, did I recognize the handful of opportunities she actually gave me to have a discussion with her about suicide, has eaten away at me for years. I've viewed not being able to recognize the warning signs of her impending death as one of my biggest failures as her mom. For parents struggling with similar situations and feelings of failure after their child's suicide, I can only say that years later, while therapy has helped me understand we do the best we can with what we know and I intellectually get it, my heart tells me otherwise. I can't help thinking I could and should have known better and done more.

It is extremely painful for bereaved parents to discover things about their child when they start digging through their belongings. They may come across writings, poetry or online activity that reveals the depth of their struggle during the time leading up to their suicide. I would tell parents that when discovering things about their child after death that they may find hard to accept, to remember it is not a reflection of their own failures. Parents aren't perfect. But neither are our kids. There is a natural tendency to idolize our deceased child.

I discovered traits in my child after her suicide that were painful to uncover. She did have a darker side. She was angry at the world. She left writings that confirmed this. Maybe she was even angry at me, though I never found any proof of this. In the end, I have to agree with the therapists who have reassured me that the suicide of any one individual is not about the failures of another. Not even the parents.

I have thought long and hard over the years about why some people (including children and young adults) choose suicide when others don't, facing the same or similar life challenges. As parents, we will always feel there was more we could and should have done for our child who has died. Attributing every suicide to mental health problems alone is not always the right answer, though it is the easiest (it lets society off the hook).

I have to consider that without any social understanding of suicide and my own struggle as a bereaved parent to understand suicide, let alone prevent it, it is natural for parents to place their own failures at the center of their child's death to obtain some kind of closure. But I don't think this is fair to parents. It is a far bigger problem.

It is only after fifteen long, difficult years in grief that I feel somewhat ready to consider that maybe my daughter's suicide really didn't have anything to do with me after all, despite the struggle I still have letting go of the belief that bringing her home would have kept her alive. I'm not so sure anymore.

Part of adopting any new thinking about the reasons for our child's death means accepting something else. In my case, that my daughter really did have problems. It doesn't matter that she was really smart, beautiful and appeared oh, so cool on the outside. She had problems that nobody around her truly understood.

No parent wants to think about their child having problems they can't understand. It makes them feel frightened and powerless. Likely, if you are reading this book you have lost your child too. Hindsight may not seem like much, except for the lessons you can learn that will one day, help you love and forgive yourself for all of your perceived failures.

Forgiveness

Forgiving you for dying, my darling daughter, was easy. I could forgive you anything. Forgiving me my failings to protect you has not been so easy.

When I think about forgiveness, I have learned that no matter how angry we get with others in our grief because of all we perceive that they have done wrong, sometimes the anger we express is really the anger we feel towards our loved one who has died. It's easy to take it out on the people closest to us. Most of the time though, we are just really angry with ourselves in grief for the many things we perceive we have done wrong. Eventually, we must learn to forgive ourselves.

Anger is based on fear. Much of the fear we feel in grief from losing our child is because of the difficulty accepting we now must live forever without the child we have lost. This is very scary to think about. It can make a parent feel resentful toward others who aren't experiencing the same pain. I know. While I have experienced several deaths since yours, none have been as painful.

For years, after losing you, sweet girl, I was terrified of everything and resented anyone who couldn't understand my grief. Seeing happy families that looked a lot like we used to, only reminded me of what I could never have again. Which was my complete family. This made me feel resentful towards them and question whether I had done something wrong to deserve losing you. Being able to forgive ourselves and others means we are ready to stop feeling resentment.

All the losses I have experienced since your death were deaths people can empathize with and know they will experience themselves one day. Losing you has always felt different. So has your suicide. Both pushed me into grief that for years, felt very frightening and isolating.

I was angry with a lot of people and wanted to blame your death on someone, which is natural after losing a child. I know now that it is naive to think that anyone, no matter what they knew or thought they knew about you, could have ever suspected what you were actually capable of; not least, predict what you would finally do. I didn't, why should they?

For a long time, the quest I was on to find a reason for your death fuelled my rage for others. Eventually, I learned to forgive whatever I judged their transgressions to be by understanding and accepting their limitations. Why can't I do that with me?

In general, I don't feel as angry anymore. I've come to realize it's pointless to hang onto such a toxic emotion. Anger isn't good for anyone to be around. It's not the way I want to live. However, I also know it can take years to fully let go of anger and resentment because both are rooted in the agonizing pain that all bereaved parents live with.

Forgiveness is steeped in compassion. It demonstrates the ability we have to rise above whatever we feel someone has done to wrong us, and what we have done to wrong ourselves or another. Lately, I have discovered that forgiveness lies more in the compassion we can feel for ourselves than only the compassion we can more easily for others. Which is making me appreciate that the journey I'm on since your death has always been more about me, than you.

Perhaps it's time I put your story away and start living my own. While I'm not entirely sure how to do this yet or if I even really want to, I do know that to make this switch in thinking, I'm going to have to genuinely forgive myself all of my perceived failings and start the next part of this journey with a clean slate.

If I knew then what I know now, I would remind newly bereaved parents that we all have limited capabilities as human beings. When it comes to the suicide of a child, there will be lots of anger and blame to go around and lots of forgiveness needed. Harmful actions and hurtful things will be done and said between loved ones. It takes time and understanding to sort through the shock of a child's death and the pain parents are feeling as the grief sets in.

While forgiveness for the self and others may still be a long way off for the newly bereaved parent, it is essential they remember not to be too hard on themselves or others when situations of anger, blame and resentment do flare up, as they will. As time marches on, they should also know that living with prolonged pain can make them do things they may later regret. It will be tempting to cling to anger, blame and resentment. However, the absence of forgiveness in grief is just another form of self-punishment. I would reassure the newly bereaved that time will give them the opportunity to see things differently. To gain a clearer perspective on all that's happened. For their heart to become a little softer.

Feeling forgiveness for others in grief likely will come sooner than being able to feel forgiveness for themselves. However, all forgiveness is a step in the right direction when it comes to healing. When it comes to forgiving others, it is important to remember that life can change on a dime. It definitely feels better to be certain that none of their relationships could suddenly end with things still left unsaid or undone.

My mother died very suddenly five years after my daughter. The first couple of years after my daughter's suicide, I had a very rocky relationship with my mom. Previously, we were close and enjoyed each other's company. When mom died, I felt so relieved that we were once again enjoying a good relationship, albeit one that was very different from what it had been. Since then I have made sure that nothing goes unsaid or undone with those I love. I never know when it will be our last phone conversation or the last time that I see them.

Finally, what I would tell anyone suffering, is that without the ability to forgive, it is certain that their healing will be hampered. Their relationships more difficult to manage. Some will collapse altogether. It is worth remembering that regardless of the pettiness and sore feelings that can linger for everyone in pain, sometimes it can be more advantageous to be the first one to forgive. Even if this is only in the stillness of their heart.

Hope

For the longest time after you died, sweet daughter, I saw only darkness all around me. I had no desire for anything. No ambition. I did not want or expect anything from anyone. I felt only a deep sense of foreboding that the worst kind of misfortune would follow me everywhere.

I remember sitting on our front porch in the first weeks after your death, gazing at the stars. I was more focused on the bits of black sky, because the stars themselves reminded me how far out of reach you had become. No matter how beautiful this scene would have been in any other circumstance, I felt only pain and impending doom, staring at the blackness.

Hope is centered on knowing what we want and feeling optimistic that things will turn out for the best. In my grief, hope eluded me time and time again as unexpected difficulties arose. Looking back, I know now I could not possibly have predicted all the challenges that lay ahead or how to cope with them in grief. I also know that this early sense of doom was my gut instinct warning me of what was to come, though there was nothing I could do to stop certain events from unfolding. It took every ounce of energy I had just to stay afloat, never mind feel hopeful for anything.

Before you died, sweet girl, my life had been driven by helping people see their full potential and finding solutions for their problems. I always encouraged them to face their difficulties, rather than run from them, and trust that everything would turn out for the best. It always did. Coping with your suicide, I had no idea how to turn that drive inward to help myself in the midst of the worst kind of personal tragedy.

There was nothing to hope for. The future looked bleak. I couldn't see a way to fix any of the problems raining down on me. I felt overwhelmed. My life and the family itself had been turned upside down. I felt it was my responsibility to figure everything out on my own. There was no one to help. Hope was not possible for me. Hope was for other people.

I've thought a lot about hope in the last few years. I've concluded that hope requires courage. You must have the courage to believe you can do or have whatever you are hoping for. Ask any parent how much hope they feel for the future after the death of their child. Ask them how much courage they have to do or go after anything. Over the years, I can't tell you how many times I've had to dig deep to find the courage just to survive. In the early years after you died, I felt betrayed by everything and everyone around me. Sometimes, even you. This left me feeling like I was drifting in a sea of despair, alone and frightened.

In photos taken of me then, I am unrecognizable. I still recall looking at myself in the mirror, feeling saddened that my mouth now drooped. My eyes appeared dull. My face was pale, thin and drawn. I didn't recognize the woman staring back at me. I didn't know who I had become.

My world had fallen apart. I was angry. I hated my life. There was no room for hope.

Until, one day, I could see a pin prick of light at the end of the dark tunnel that had consumed my thoughts and mind. As tiny as it was, I remember it clearly. While I had no idea how long it would take for me to crawl through the darkness or even if I could eventually reach this light, it gave me the hope I needed to hang on. To keep going until I could believe and trust that one day, I would be able to reach for more than what I could only at that moment. Trusting you would always be by my side in some way, I started to feel a stirring of hope that things in my life could be better. I started to move.

If I knew then what I know now, I would gently warn newly bereaved parents that they can expect a long, hard journey, but there will be much they will learn along the way. Remembering to take tiny steps and embracing the encouragement of loved ones, little by little they can trust that they will put their life back together again.

That they move slowly and even take turns that feel all wrong at times, isn't the point. Each small success will take them one step closer to where they want to go.

Finding a sliver of hope in whatever way they can as early as possible in grief will help them trust there can be more to life than only pain. Having said this, hope is not something that can be forced. It will come in stages. It will come and go. The momentary excitement that always accompanies new awareness can just as quickly be overthrown by setbacks that are common in grief from child loss. They should remember all setbacks are temporary. They will find equilibrium again.

I would also tell newly bereaved parents to feel assured that hope can and will provide them comfort. It will lift them out of darker moods. It is the compass they so desperately need when they feel as though they've fallen by the wayside. It will help them discover who they are now and who they want to become.

Hope is eternal. If nothing else and if only for today, all they can hope for is to find the strength and courage to accept their life as it has become, this will be enough to help them start believing and trusting that one day, they can feel certain there will be so much more.

Acceptance

Acceptance is a loaded word for me. There are many things in my life I can accept, but your death, dear daughter, still isn't one of them. Oh, I can accept that you are no longer physically alive. To do otherwise would not be rational. In my grief, though I struggled to have rational thoughts in the beginning years, this period of insanity that all bereaved parents feel did eventually leave me. I stopped looking for you. Reaching for you. Waiting for you to call or walk through the front door at any moment. In a way, this was the sign of me intellectually accepting your death, however much my heart rebelled.

How I have struggled through the years to accept your death in every other way. What bereaved parent, or any griever for that matter coping with sudden loss, doesn't struggle to accept their new reality? One they have been thrown into without warning. Maybe I am stuck more in this and the choice you made to die, rather than the actual death itself.

To accept something, we must understand it for its truth. The circumstance or offering must hold meaning for us that cannot be challenged. Anything we feel reluctant to accept is certain to create adverse fallout. Tell me, in what reality would it be easy or even reasonable for me to accept your choice to die? Or to find value and meaning in an act I never could condone? I do not understand, nor have I been able to find any real meaning in your suicide or the pain I have been left with.

I have struggled long and hard with my challenge to accept your death and my loss. I wonder if they even are the same. Focusing only on my loss shifts all accountability for my struggle from your own experience of dying to my experience in grief. A nuance, perhaps, but still powerful when you consider more closely, the difference.

I sometimes wonder if I were to mentally and emotionally let go of my obsession with your death, whether this would heal me of considerable pain. Without tying almost all of my thoughts and emotions to that final act of your life; your death, perhaps I would get to choose more how I wanted to live my life. In or out of grief. But if I could even do this, there remains the question of whether or not this wouldn't be doing you a great disservice.

I have always intended to honor you for all you meant to me and others when you were alive. Not to think or even talk about your death doesn't make sense to me. It seems I would have to put all the pieces that remain of you, which are my memories, in some type of box in my brain and close the lid. Close with some finality, all those chapters of my life that included you. How would I do this? How could I?

This is a conundrum I have yet to solve. I have talked to therapists and read books on grief. No one yet has provided me with a satisfactory answer as to how I could accept your death and all it has meant and be okay with it.

It's not just your death I've had difficulty accepting. There are many other things. Not least, the dreams I had for you. For the family. All of which I feel I've been robbed of. At times, it is very difficult for me to appreciate the joys my contemporaries are experiencing becoming grandparents and celebrating the milestones of *all* their children. They don't have to hide away the memories of a child.

It's been hard for me to accept the way my life turned out, despite how well your brother is doing and the joy I've felt from all his accomplishments. I had different plans in mind that included *all of us*. That I may be remembered mostly for my broken heart is heart breaking. I could tell myself a million times over that your death was worth every lesson and the spiritual growth I have enjoyed, but I'm not sure that's true. In fact, I don't think it is. I'd give it all up in a heartbeat just to have you back.

If I knew then what I know now, I would tell newly bereaved parents that meaning, and acceptance go hand in hand. Without finding meaning for their child's suicide, parents are presented with one of the biggest struggles in grief. Which is accepting their child's death.

For years, I thought that the grief I was experiencing from my daughter's suicide was different than what other parents were experiencing from losing their child some other way. It was going on too long. I must have been impacted and suffering in a way I didn't understand. But from all I've read about grief related to child loss and the bereaved parents I've met I know this simply isn't true. Grief from child loss is the same for everyone, despite the many different reasons our children die. However, without an explanation to help us understand why our child *chose* their death, accepting their death is very difficult. It can keep us searching for answers and tie us to the traumatic event itself. Often for years.

While many bereaved parents can find purpose and meaning for their life after their child's passing and do good in the world with what they've learned, I have yet to meet one parent that has found total peace after their child's death, no matter what they're doing. That doesn't mean they're not out there. Only that I haven't met them. And while finding cures for diseases, raising awareness for organ donation or implementing new laws from certain types of accidents are causes that can be healing for the parent, and often bring about great social discourse and change, suicide is different.

Suicide is uncomfortable for most people to think about, let alone talk about. It is impossible for anyone to understand. The deaths are always secretive. They are almost always violent. It goes against human nature for parents to imagine their children being capable of killing themselves. When our kids do die, parents are left, often for years, traumatized by the horrendous images and thoughts about the months, weeks, days, hours and moments leading right up to their child committing that one final self-destructive act, which also represents the destruction of everything else in their life.

How are we supposed to accept all of this? I'm not sure we can. Instead, I would suggest to parents it may be easier to focus on the things they can accept, rather than trying to force themselves to accept something they never can or aren't ready to accept. I know. I've tried. It was a futile exercise that only brought me greater angst than what I was experiencing giving in to what I was really feeling.

For newly bereaved parents, I would also reassure them that the acceptance of the smallest things here and there in early grief will lead them to the acceptance of more challenging issues later on in grief. This includes acceptance of their changing capabilities, loss of former interests and changing relationships. All of which are a normal part of grief.

Finally, I would say that acceptance requires their willingness. It is necessary for bereaved parents to periodically step away from everything that is distracting and spend time quietly contemplating their life, the situation that is challenging them and what they want.

Accepting that their life will never be the way they once imagined it represents a huge turning point. It is a sign that the acceptance of other things is sure to follow.

Envy

I recently heard someone caution about envy and asked myself if I still didn't envy others who had not lost their child. Not that I'd want them to. My first reaction was to deny I'd ever had this feeling when you first died, sweet daughter. But the truth is, I think I have felt a little envious of those who can't relate to my loss experience. It's not just your dying, but your suicide. It's without doubt, part of the reason why I have felt so isolated in my grief.

Your suicide brought considerable distress to my life. How much I've been knocked around in grief compared to those who can still enjoy the numerous advantages of a complete family has weighed heavily on my mind over the years. Reaping the rewards of the joys and certain contentment that comes from watching all your children grow and prosper. Maybe even taking the family for granted, as oblivious as I once was to the perils of what could befall them.

Anything to do with mothers and daughters is the worst for me. Never again will I get to enjoy that enviable bond that many moms and daughters do or know that pure peace and contentment of a family all together. There is always that one piece missing. You!

Naturally, to think about other people who can enjoy this does still make me a little envious, truth be told. Not as envious as earlier years in my bereavement, but envy is still there to some degree.

Not taking anything away from the joy I do feel with our little family of three (I love your brother dearly), I still feel a little off-kilter with you gone. Like I've been balancing on a rather tall pole on one foot for too long.

The whole family misses you. I think everyone is a little off balance. Your absence is noticeable in everything we do. Everywhere we go. We are missing out not having you with us.

As a mom, it doesn't feel natural to have one of my kids gone from the picture. I can't imagine it ever will. I think about what you would be doing now. How far you might have gone in your life (you always were a little ahead of your time). What you would look like now. It's hard not to feel a bit envious of those who can boast about all their grown children's accomplishments and have the photos to prove it.

No one has forgotten about you. Just because your brother may not talk about you, he listens when I do. I know he's been impacted terribly by your death. He no longer has his big sis!

I can still remember how one of you felt when you achieved something or had a milestone to celebrate. The other one got just as excited. And I'll always remember that Mother's Day when you both cooked me dinner. My heart was in my mouth with all the banging pots and pans and orders flying around, but the laughter from you both kept me seated right where I was. I knew then that this would be a forever memory. Little did I know what forever would actually come to mean.

How proud I was of each of you. You both filled me to my core with joy. It took me years after your death before I could utter congratulations to anyone.

If I knew then what I know now, I would tell newly bereaved parents that envy is a natural part of grief. It comes from the pain we feel from the worst loss of all: our child. How could we not envy others who have what for us, represents loss of such magnitude?

I would also tell newly bereaved parents that all painful emotions in grief are fleeting. They will come and go. While often they will be heightened and sometimes more muted, one thing is certain: of the tens of dozens there are, though hidden perhaps, many will remain lurking just under the surface and will surprise them with their intensity. As one of them, opportunities will abound for envy to flare up the more grieving parents put themselves out there.

One of the hardest things to experience in grief is the stark realization that normal life goes on for everyone around the griever, and quickly too. This includes extended family. For the bereaved parent though, their world will feel as though it has completely stopped. There will be chaos, disruptions, feuding and endless pain. Misunderstandings can cause rifts between family members and friends. Relationships often end when people no longer can or want to be part of the suffering. Early grief is one of the most isolating periods where this can be intensely felt; a period I suggest lasts around three years.

Where family relationships and friendships do remain intact, there will be many happy occasions for lots of other people to celebrate through the years. Children's graduations. Their budding careers and promotions. Engagements. Weddings. The birth of babies. Any bereaved parent can quickly become overwhelmed feeling they have to attend any type of celebratory event. Envy may well top the list of reasons they don't want to go.

Finally, I would say to the newly bereaved parent, it can take many firsts and lots of time to sort out what they feel they can and cannot do. What they do or do not like any longer. Disruptions of this sort and those described above are inevitable throughout grief. Parents must watch that their surviving children do not get caught up in any feelings of ostracization or feuding with others, especially when they are younger. They may even separate the family grief entirely from their school and social life to protect themselves. Our son did this from age thirteen. It continues to this day. While I didn't understand it then, I do now.

Willingness

I have never associated willingness with being cheerful, yet, there is that association. So, I am wondering, sweet daughter, if the reason I feel so resistant towards willingness at times, which is critical in grief, is because I lack all cheerfulness. It certainly would change my perspective of suffering and overall experience in my bereavement.

If cheerfulness is an inherent part of one's nature, as I think it is (either you are born with it or you're not), it's safe to say I never really was a cheerful person, though I've always had a great sense of humor. I was the serious one. The worrier. How could I possibly will myself to cheerfully do anything in the aftermath of your suicide? I've often wondered whether my personality type has put me at a distinct disadvantage in my grief to those who always choose to look at life more positively.

While once in a while I can feel a lightness to my being, this is rare. In grief, I'm still the serious one. The worrier. Though I'm grateful I can laugh again and appreciate a good belly roar now and then, laughter is not something I've enjoyed as much as I did before. In fact, I can still remember the first time I really laughed four years after you died. The sound that emerged from my belly was as foreign to me as if I was spitting up some weird object. I felt the same way when I caught myself humming a little tune too, right around the same time.

It was then I noticed that maybe I could be a little more willing to think differently about your death. About my grief. About my future.

To possess willingness is a great gift. In grief, it gives us a more positive outlook on life. On our relationships. On our potential and possibilities.

Willingness is also related to being eager and ready. To seize opportunities. To change what we are no longer satisfied with in life. To feel alive and create new dreams.

However, as wonderful as all this sounds, without you by my side I often feel incapable of diving right into all of my potential and embracing all the possibilities. Not that I can't manage without you. I've demonstrated that I can. But, with you gone, how much of me really exists, or to what extent I could ever feel fully alive again, remains questionable. I've questioned this a lot over the years. It is the reason for all my starts and stops and inability to have the world by its tail once again.

If I knew then what I know now, I would tell newly bereaved parents that any willingness they feel to make changes in their grief must first, serve them well. They should feel reassured that one day, they will find within themselves the willingness to want their life to be different.

The focus of any change should not be on what they believe others expect of them or what they may be demanding of themselves (a return to work too soon, taking on added responsibility, getting back to their "old self"). Change must come from their heart and when they know they can handle any fallout.

There will be many false starts trying anything new in grief. It is always evolving. The willingness one individual may feel to change anything in their life should take into account the readiness of loved ones to change anything in their own. Where appropriate, everyone's concerns should be discussed with regard to any of the changes that may or will affect them.

Whether experiencing parent bereavement as a grieving partner, parent to surviving children, adult son or daughter, sister or brother, those new to their bereavement should remain on guard for changes in all of their relationships and ability to meet certain obligations. All relationships need to be managed in grief by the very nature that a person is different who is now bereaved. It is therefore necessary for newly bereaved parents to help loved ones understand that while they may not know who they now are, they no longer are the person they once were. While this can be devastating for family members to accept, relationships can become stronger and even better than before.

As an example, right after my daughter died, I had to stop going to my mom's place for what had been regular family dinners. The pain of seeing my daughter's empty chair was just too much for me. As a result of my child's death, the relationship between my mom and I changed considerably. Instead of dinners, I had sporadic and short visits with her at her home instead. Eventually, and only after a few years when I began to go out socially, I would meet or take her for coffee where we had wonderful visits. Though my mom was likely deeply saddened by all this and I know for certain she was by the changes in me, when she died suddenly in 2010, we had the best relationship we could possibly have under the circumstances. I was grateful that nothing had been left unsaid between us before her passing.

All of my changes in grief have only come about as a result of me being willing to take that next step, wherever it was leading me. In the early years, this meant redefining all of my relationships to save them. I actually told all of my loved ones how I had changed and what they could expect of me. I became willing to take responsibility for what I wanted to experience in grief instead of what others were doing in their own, which remains true to this day. I had to become willing to be brave and grow, when I really didn't want to, and support loved ones in their grief when I knew no one could help me in my own.

I would suggest that when newly bereaved parents are ready to make changes in their grief, they do so in the best interests of their healing and based on what is important to them at that moment. Change of any type, even of one's beliefs, can create fallout. It is essential that grieving parents as partners never assume anything about each other. That family members are honest with each other as they heal together. That no one individual feels pressured to do anything because of somebody else's expectations. And, that all family members feel free and safe enough to explore their evolving feelings, even when this may lead to changes that may make some family members feel uncomfortable.

Finally, I would tell the newly bereaved that behind every act of willingness is the opportunity to create something new. It is not possible to stay completely stagnant in grief. While it is true that the early years of grief feel unbearable for every bereaved parent, it does change over time. While it may not ever go away, somehow, we all learn to go on living. Willingness is the almost automatic response every bereaved parent acquires in their desire to feel better and want more for their life, wherever they are in their grief.

Longing

L onging means to crave or desire something that is unattainable. You certainly are that, dear daughter. Because we are expected to replace our longing for a loved one with our memories of happier times, the standard reply for many people trying to comfort those of us stricken by grief is to remind us that we still have our memories. Translated, this means we should be grateful for the time we had with our loved one, which is much easier said than done. No grieving parent wants to hear that. Likely, nobody does who is suffering from any loss.

Years ago, right after you died, when my longing for you felt intolerable, many people offering their condolences mentioned something to me about my memories. Every time the word was uttered, or I read it in a card verse, I was left reeling. I was angry that anyone would have the nerve, either via a card or in person, to tell me what to do with my memories. In fact, many of my memories left me after you died. I still can only grab at little pieces here and there trying to remember what life was like before your death.

In those early days, my longing for you was intense: not least that your death never happened in the first place. I thought I would lose my mind with you gone. I felt helpless and desperate to find you, like a caged lioness separated from her cub. It took many months, if not a couple of years, for my longing for your physical presence to subside. It probably saved me that I stayed focused on my spiritual studies to try and gain an understanding of your death that in the physical realm, was just not possible.

My longing for you today comes more from my continual struggle to honor your time on this planet. I wish that things were different so that I could talk more openly about you. When I feel I can't talk about you at all, it's like you never existed. Like most bereaved parents, I long to talk about you, despite the fact you aren't physically here anymore.

The reality is that talking about your death either makes people feel uncomfortable or upsets them. Besides not knowing what to say, it reminds them too much of what's at stake thinking about their own family. I've found that talking with people about my loss without sharing any details about your death is one thing. Talking about your suicide heightens their discomfort. Generally, I now only talk about your brother when asked how many kids I have, except on those rare occasions when I feel I can share more.

Every time I can't talk about you, I feel I'm being dishonest with myself and others. For many years, the silence I've endured around child loss, suicide and my bereavement has denied me the ability to speak the truth about what's rightfully mine. My story. It has also complicated and maybe even prolonged my grief.

There is an obvious social problem when talking about child loss and grief feels this unnatural and so unwelcoming. I can't tell you how comforting it feels just to sit with another bereaved parent. Even when the words are few, much is always shared in the silence.

While today I no longer feel the same longing to have you back, because I can accept that you are physically gone, I do still long for other things. To heal my broken heart. To feel satisfied doing what I'm doing for the time I have left on this planet.

I used to feel immense longing for our story to have turned out differently. To one where the ending is still being written. While

I may not pine away the hours longing for all I can accept is just not possible, I've discovered there is a difference between longing and my sadness that may never go away.

If I knew then what I know now, I'd tell newly bereaved parents to brace themselves for the longing they will undoubtedly feel in the absence of their child. As painful as it is, longing is a natural part of the grief. To feel less alone, they may want to talk with and read books written by other bereaved parents who are willing to share their experiences in grief. This help can be especially comforting in the early months and years when the longing feels more intense.

Longing for a deceased child, I expect feels much like losing a limb, where the sensation of that limb remains where once it was attached. All of us as bereaved parents, feel an ongoing attachment to and longing for our lost child through our heart and spirit. This produces physical sensations where we may think we see them. We wait for them to call or come home. We believe they are still with us. We obsess over their personal belongings and make shrines of their bedrooms and other areas of the home. It feels painful to even think about giving anything up.

Longing is something that will dissipate on its own. I'd gently caution newly bereaved parents to remember that they cannot force themselves to feel any emotion in grief. Longing for their child is something they will experience as a normal part of grief. It will subside over time and as they become more accepting of their loss.

Choice

Choice: now that's a weighted word. I won't even attempt to revisit the many choices I could have made differently when you were still alive, sweet daughter. Instead, I'll stick to contemplating those I can be making right here and now that would serve me best.

Up to this point, looking back in my grief and thinking about the choices I've made, thoughts about what I could or should have done differently have challenged me. Some have even left me with a terrible sense of guilt. In the early years, I often felt I should be doing more to get over my pain from losing you. If not for me, then for others. It's time to change all that.

There are so many choices that must be made throughout grief to help us slog our way through the pain. Some decisions I felt pushed into making in the early months and years based on circumstance alone. Others, and much later in my grief, I began to make with more clarity and planning going into my decision. Something that has lasted to this day. Consistently though, with every one of my choices, bad or good, made out of necessity or desire, I've considered what would be best for my healing, even when I didn't know where the next step would take me.

In the earlier years, without insight or sometimes even rational thinking, every choice I made was to help me feel less worse than what I was already feeling. Fast forward fifteen years, and in looking back at the first five I consider to be my early grief; years that threw me the worst of my troubles, I wish I'd known more about trauma. I'm certain this would have helped me avoid making some of the choices I did based solely on my instinct to survive. There was no thought that went into any of them. Though they always turned out okay, my anxiety and feeling I was endlessly grabbing at straws did nothing to help me gain a clearer sense of where I was heading, or where I wanted to go throughout this entire period. Every choice I made was a gut reaction to get me out of one difficult situation after another. It was exhausting.

Given my total lack of knowledge about grief in these early years, I do believe now there is nothing I could have done differently then, to make my life less miserable or difficult. I'm thankful they are behind me. I've never again experienced anything as harsh. Today, while I wish I'd had the courage in the beginning of my grief to put more thought into what I really needed and wanted, rather than always having a knee-jerk reaction to every disruption that came my way, hindsight taught me there is always more than one solution for any challenge. Everything always gets resolved. However, feeling panicked as we do when living with trauma, we can't see this. We only want the problem gone. The suffering to end. Eventually, and as I gained a clearer sense of my needs, over the next few years I started to make decisions with more confidence, focusing on the outcome I wanted for my life.

I have learned there is no point in looking only in the rearview mirror to gauge where I am at any point in my grief. Grief is fluid. Punishing myself for decisions I once made that today I would make differently only keeps me stuck in pain. It serves no real purpose.

I can see now that every single choice I made in earlier years was designed to get me somewhere that I wasn't. While it's not easy revisiting in my mind the burden I carried to ensure the family would survive; that I would survive, perhaps it's time now to think more about the strength it took for me to lead us all right where we are today.

I've learned that letting go of all the what if's after losing a child is hard. At some point, it is better to remember just how tough this journey is for anyone traveling the road of parent bereavement and feel proud of every step we take to move forward. In my heart, I believe and can accept I've always done the best I could in grief with the knowledge that I've had. There really aren't mistakes in grief.

There is one thing I do still think a lot about though, regarding choice. That is, whether healing is as simple as choosing to relinquish all one's pain. If in choosing not to do so, we are instead choosing only to keep punishing ourselves for any death for which we feel we are to blame. Specifically, my darling daughter, if I could accept your death was not my fault and let go of all my suffering, would this make it then okay that you are gone? I don't think I could live with that.

I've read countless books, talked with therapists and struggled with my conscience for years to find an answer to this question. I've concluded there can be no suffering on its own. *We* give it life. Would it not make sense then, that it remains our choice to continue suffering or not? Is healing in our acceptance of one's death alone?

There is this notion that powerful lessons can be learned from suffering. This has certainly been true for me. Yet, if this is the case, would it not also be true that the same can be said for choosing to live healed? That so many of us keep ourselves living in a state of pain must be for some reason.

If I knew then what I know now, I'd tell newly bereaved parents that second-guessing all their choices prior to their child's death and blaming themselves for their child's suicide is common in grief. They are likely to obsess about all the signs they missed. The choices they could and should have made differently. That by having done just one thing differently they could have saved their child's life. It's a grueling and exhausting form of self-punishment. Finding no answers and coping with the agony from knowing they will never get another chance to do anything over again, only adds to the trauma.

I have found over the years, that what we do as parents raising our children is not much different than what we do getting through grief after losing them. It can take years to accept the bad choices we've made when anything does go wrong in life. The suicide of our child can represent the ultimate in our failures. Mine have haunted me for years.

Only now, am I able to take a more objective look at my choices as a mom prior to my child's suicide (in grief, none have felt so egregious). Because it's been very painful to let go of my belief that somehow, I was responsible for my daughter not wanting to live, rethinking all the things I did or said that may have been wrong when at the time they all felt right, has been confusing. It's only from the objectivity that time has given me, I've been able to consider letting go of all those things that no longer are serving any purpose.

I would encourage grieving parents to remember that because they can't change anything from the past, when looking back at anything for which they feel remorse, having some objectivity will help them find the patience, love and kindness for themselves that is necessary for their healing.

Understanding that ultimately what they choose to let go of or keep in pain will always be up to them, it may be comforting to remember that with the introspection they will acquire and the knowledge they will gain in grief, both can be trusted as a guiding force to get them through the pain.

Pain

What can I say about pain, sweet child? I've spent years trying to understand human pain and suffering. In a very general sense, the two are connected, but different. I view pain as that which we identify from the physical diseases and injuries we acquire. People are quick to empathize with those who are experiencing any discomfort, distress and agony associated with physical pain. Our symptoms are diagnosed, treated and healing is expected to occur based on the prognosis provided.

Suffering is a state we *endure* that arises from a painful experience. The symptoms are not always obvious. For grieving parents, they are highly complex. The pain is difficult to understand, not only for those experiencing it, but for those trying to provide support. Because both are so complex, I'll focus here on pain and speak about suffering on its own.

It is only years after your death, darling daughter, that I have come to understand physical pain more intimately. From the moment you died, my body was wracked with a pain I've never felt before or since, from anything else. While it wasn't obvious to those who didn't know me, those who did immediately recognized how different I had instantly become in my bereavement.

For years, I felt frustrated and angry that I had to hide how much pain I was in. I had to force myself to act normal in so many situations, which did nothing for my healing. In fact, it only added to the pesky illnesses I did endure here and there that quickly became chronic, and eventually wore me out. It was at this moment of collapse, ten years after you died, that I began to pay a lot more attention to my body in pain. I found I could no longer lean only on the spiritual experience of my loss to help me understand all of what I was going through in grief.

I decided to dive deep into what was happening to me physically as a result of my ongoing emotional pain. I became more aware of trauma triggers and how my body was reacting (physical illness, distress, collapse). I immediately started to change what wasn't working in my life to start creating the balance I needed in both mind and body, if I was to have any chance at all of making a full recovery from what was decidedly now, a disability.

While there have been many bumps along the way through this journey of grief, as there are for every bereaved parent, since the start of this last turning point in my life five years ago, I can feel that things are finally starting to change. Despite the various limitations I live with as a result of acquiring Post-Traumatic Stress Disorder (I have far less energy and still cope with chronic illness), it has been freeing to understand all of who I am in grief. This deeper insight has guided me to only make choices that will help me live healthier all around.

Initially, while I moved across the country, downsized, cleared away a lot of material stuff, retired from my job and pared down my obligations considerably, none of these changes were necessarily easy or happened overnight. Each one represented another step that has led me to where I now feel more relaxed and in charge of my life.

Though the pain of losing you remains, precious child, accepting it as part of me has made me realize how pointless it is to try and force pain to go away. It's far easier and more realistic to accept emotional pain as part of my life now. Because it has depleted my energy in so many ways, I've had to learn to manage my life one day at a time, and in accordance with whatever is happening in the moment or how I am feeling in general.

My goal is no longer to get rid of pain altogether, no matter how much I would prefer this. I've found the inner struggle to try and be something I'm not, exhausting. Not succeeding at overcoming my pain doesn't mean I've failed at healing. It simply means I'm living my life the best way I can, despite my pain from losing you. It doesn't matter where I am on the journey to heal. The important thing is I'm on the journey; and moving.

One of the most important lessons I learned when I began to dig deeper into my physical experience in grief, was just how debilitating my emotional pain had been on my body. It literally knocked me off my feet. To that point, I hadn't realized how much I had been stretching myself beyond my limits. I missed all the signs of my impending collapse. Until, one morning I couldn't move. It felt like another ending of me. And, in a way, it was.

This collapse in 2015 birthed the latest version of me in grief. One that will continue to evolve because I now know how to better manage my life, not try to overhaul it. To always put my needs in healing first. To have fun exploring who I am becoming. That effort counts as much as the end result.

If I knew then what I know now, I'd tell newly bereaved parents to give themselves a huge pat on the back right out of the gate just for having to take that first step into grief. It is an arduous journey that no bereaved parent would ever wish on others, despite knowing the same heartache will always await somebody else. For any parent, this makes me sad. For those of us losing children to suicide, even more so. When I contemplate the enormity of my own loss from my daughter literally, ending her life, I am still, at times, without words. I feel great compassion for what I know every new bereaved parent will go through experiencing the same thing, which is part of what drives me to help in any way I can.

I'd tell those new to grief there will be pain, and lots of it. I have yet to meet a bereaved parent where their suffering hasn't been etched on their face and in their eyes. Their body language is always just a little bit different. They remind me of me.

Today, I feel fortunate to understand the symbiosis between the emotional pain of grief and the impact it has had on my body. I would caution others to be aware early on that lasting emotional pain from the shock and trauma of losing their child can have devastating effects on their body. They should seek medical help as soon as possible for any ongoing symptoms, even if this means educating their doctor about all aspects of their grief.

There are countless stories of grieving parents developing a wide range of illnesses and symptoms for which there is no diagnosis. The same thing happened to me. For years, various doctors put my physical symptoms down to stress, until I was finally diagnosed with Post-Traumatic Stress Disorder in 2014.

While nothing can take away the pain from losing a child, there are things grieving parents can do to find some comfort and feel supported, starting early in their grief. They can establish an online and/or in-person support network. They can encourage sharing within the family about what every family member is feeling and experiencing in grief and find ways to support each other in their individual and family pain. If they have returned to work, they can discuss work accommodations that may be available to better support them at the various stages of their recovery. I arranged a combination of work alternatives for years before my disability.

As a griever, they should become familiar with their rights regarding health benefits and employment insurance. While this will vary between countries, I found after my PTSD diagnosis that people and employers were genuinely concerned and wanted to help me.

Bereaved parents should not be afraid to see their doctor to discuss their health issues, no matter how silly they think they are. I was terrified to see my doctor because it was very difficult for me to ask for help. Newly bereaved parents may feel the same way. Looking back, I can confidently say that all of my illnesses were grief related, simply because my immune system had been so weakened. It left me then and still does, vulnerable to frequent bouts of ill-health, which I'm trying to change.

It is important that bereaved parents take care of themselves. I met many in my early grief who years later in their own, still weren't comfortable with doing anything to soothe themselves. I always did from the beginning. Some examples of self-care include taking a bubble bath by candlelight, resting, meditating, doing gentle exercise, getting fresh air, enjoying a cup of tea with a good friend, buying fresh flowers. Whatever small pleasure they once enjoyed can be comforting to try again, in moderation.

Newly bereaved parents should take care they don't plan to do too much too soon. It takes time to adjust to grief. Part of this will be discovering what they can and can't handle. What they may or may not enjoy anymore. They will find they have changed considerably. Additionally, and because trauma does some strange things to the mind, they may find themselves thinking and doing things that seem not "normal" in early grief. For months I wanted to clean out all our household furniture and stare only at bare walls. I couldn't take anything I perceived as clutter, around me. Because this wasn't practical, instead I retreated to my two favorite rooms in our home and spent hours alone reading, writing, resting and meditating. Eventually, I did feel ready for more.

Seeing loved ones in pain is uncomfortable for loved ones and friends. Because of this, newly bereaved parents can expect some relationships to fall by the wayside. Some may bounce back. Others may end for good. They can feel reassured that as their life does pick up again, they will meet new friends. Have wonderful relationships. Return to activities or find new ones they enjoy. In all of this though, I've found it is the bereaved parent who must adapt to the world of "normal". After fifteen years of being a bereaved mom, this hasn't changed. I've learned to accept that because no one can take a parent's pain away from losing their child, if we want a life outside our grief, we have to adapt to what feels normal for others. This can be frustrating. It can cause anxiety, discomfort, and more pain.

Newly bereaved parents must allow their re-entry into any aspect of their former life to be measured. There will be many things they discover about themselves in grief through this process alone. They must follow their heart and instinct in whatever they choose to do, regardless of any pressure they may feel from others or their nagging conscience.

Ultimately, I would tell all bereaved parents that in whatever way we experience pain, I've found that most people hang tight to it. They either don't understand pain or they want to ignore it altogether. In my own bereavement and in helping others, I recognize the courage it takes to face our pain head on. I also know that when we don't, it will catch up with us one way or another at some point.

I've met people whose lives were destroyed from holding onto their pain from grief. Without my spiritual practice, I'm sure that would have been true for me, too. It took me ten years to find the courage to put my spiritual crutch away for a time, to take a hard look at me in only flesh and bone. It felt confusing, frightening and required changes of me I didn't know I had the strength to make.

I've found the key to living with pain from grief, yet still feel confident we are moving towards whatever recovery is possible, is dependent on three things:

1. Accepting pain as part of our life.
2. Deciding at any point, how much we want to remain living in pain.
3. Doing what we can to heal throughout the various stages of our grief.

Suffering

It may well be that suffering is a fool's friend. Suffering is a state we *endure* that arises from a painful experience. It is a state of pain we bear without resistance. We may or may not know we are suffering, but one thing is certain: without understanding it, suffering can be difficult, if not impossible, to overcome. We first must understand the pain that has caused our suffering if we are ever to decide if we may even be willing to overcome it.

Suffering related to the loss of a child is complicated. While all deaths of our children are traumatic, our child's death from suicide leaves us, as parents bewildered, overwhelmed, stigmatized and searching for answers that are impossible to find. This unending searching makes our grief complex and our pain a state that is quick to become suffering that feels incurable.

When I contemplate my suffering, darling girl, the questions I most often ask are: What value has suffering brought me? Is suffering what I want to experience the rest of my life? If not, what can I do to live more joyfully? If I were at my end and reviewing my life, would I see suffering as a major theme? If yes, can I change this? (Surely, I don't want to live a life centered only on suffering.) What lessons have I learned from your death that would allow me to relinquish all my suffering? What would I replace it with? If relinquishing my suffering is not possible, then what quality of life will I have?

In this searching I concluded that if I was to fully understand my suffering, I had to understand all of my pain. In doing so, I discovered I've been saddled with limitations from the onslaught of my bereavement that have drastically altered my life; some that are likely to remain a part of me (which has been difficult to accept given my former feisty self). As such, my assumption about suffering has been tested. Earlier in my grief, I had different ideas about who I could become that fooled me into believing suffering may boil down to personal choice. Today I'm not so sure. As with everything in grief, I've had to reconsider or change my thinking many times.

Today, and with respect to child loss, I'm finding that relinquishing suffering is not quite so simple. Accepting suffering as a natural part of my bereavement has helped me become more discerning in my grief. It's helped me create the type of environments that I want and need to be in. The type of people I want to surround myself with. The type of work I want to do in a way that supports my current state of health. I never again want to feel I have to pretend to be more than who I really am.

Though much has been written about suffering as a human condition, before your death, I didn't think too much about it. Like most people, I was sensitive to suffering in general. Since your death, I've spent countless hours contemplating whether suffering really is a necessary part of the human condition; and if so, is it useful only as a means to help us choose light over dark? I know this sounds somewhat biblical, but in it myself for so long, I can't see any other reason for so much suffering in the world. I won't deny I've felt mostly darkness since you died. Pursuing a light-filled life has always been at the center of my healing efforts. It is doubtful I ever would have attained the healing and spiritual growth I have without this level of suffering. But equally, I can attest that all my changes have been based on personal choice alone. Which really only demonstrates just how complicated suffering is and leaves me right back where I started. Wondering whether suffering is a choice or not. Perhaps it is our state of mind that can be influenced and conditioned to make us think and reason differently that would take our suffering away. But it would still remain our choice to do this.

Alternatively, it may be that suffering is of no use at all. That, as mere mortals, we are simply fooling ourselves (I can imagine you smiling at this, dear daughter, from wherever you now are). Given it's doubtful anyone on this planet truly knows what it would be like to live free from all suffering, I can only imagine it would require we attain a constant state of inner peace and certain detachment to our physical existence. While this may be possible to some degree with effort on an individual scale, there still is the obvious difficulty humans have in general to understand, let alone feel compassion for their personal suffering, never mind the suffering of the world. Which suggests to me that as a species we are nowhere near the point where we would choose to end it.

I'd suggest any detachment we have to suffering allows us to create a false sense of safety that we think protects us from the same or similar fate as those we know really are suffering. Is this because left with suffering on our own, we wouldn't know what to do with it? I certainly don't.

We are woefully ill-equipped to deal with any of the fallout when tragedy strikes. People can only identify with someone else's suffering if they have experienced it themselves. I feel I've hit a brick wall trying to find answers that would help me ease the suffering I've endured for years after losing you, sweet girl. No one really knows what to do with it for the simple fact that the answers must come from within.

I truly believe I am responsible for whatever state I want to be in. Ending my suffering still tops the list of things I'd like to change about my life. This would no doubt bring me the peace I want. But somehow, my daughter, even in contemplating my desire to free myself of all my suffering, I feel uncertain about what this actually means. Deep down I fear it would mean losing you all over again. In a different way, but still losing you again.

If I knew then what I know now, I would tell everyone, bereaved or not, there is nothing any of us can do to prepare for the suicide of a child or other loved one. I feel great empathy and compassion for every parent and other loved one grieving a suicide. While these writings focus on my experience as a bereaved parent, I feel the same sensitivity and sorrow for every suicide survivor, no matter what their relationship was to the deceased, because of the terrible guilt and regret that accompanies every suicide at some level.

It is easy to quickly fall into a pattern of self-torture when we believe we should have seen the suicide coming and done something more to prevent it. I'm certain everyone affected by a suicide feels this to some degree. For a parent losing their child, there are no words to describe the depth to which we suffer guilt, regret and sorrow for not having done more to help them. I still struggle with this after all these years.

In looking back to my early grief and all that I didn't know, I would certainly caution newly bereaved parents today to educate themselves about trauma and the problems that trauma alone contributes to prolonged suffering. Without doubt, it impacts personal relationships and every other area of the griever's life. Being forewarned about the real and potential harm of trauma in grief after child loss, will allow bereaved parents to find the support they need as soon as possible, to work through the difficulties that trauma brings to already complex grief. These troubles will become more challenging and complex if left untreated. There are therapists trained in treating trauma that I am certain can help bereaved parents as much as anyone else who has been traumatized, though the approach would likely have to be modified to address issues specific to the grief we experience after child loss.

I never knew about trauma or Post-Traumatic Stress Disorder (PTSD) in the first two years of my grief. By the time I started to research trauma on the internet in 2007, I still could only wonder how I may have been impacted by trauma or even had PTSD from the shock of my child's suicide. I could not find any information on trauma in grief. It wasn't until 2014 that I discovered I had been suffering from PTSD since the onset of my bereavement in 2005. I am certain that therapies practiced today (such as compassion focused therapy) could have helped me dodge or at least manage more effectively much of the collateral damage I'm still trying to fix had I'd been more informed, and they'd been available.

All grieving parents need ongoing support, but they also need insight and the energy to search out the right therapist and therapy. Additionally, not everyone has the finances or insurance to attend therapy. Many bereaved parents (me included) avoid seeking help in early grief for other reasons. As newly bereaved parents we are angry, frightened and haven't got a clue what we need. It can take years to sort through the broken pieces of our life.

While circumstances in grief will change, the core of our suffering cannot. At least, not until we know for certain what is causing us to suffer. To free ourselves, perhaps it does come down to eventually, being able to feel compassion for ourselves, and learning to love and accept all those things about our character that otherwise, we are so quick to judge.

Anger

Anger is a devastating emotion. We get angry with others when we feel they have wronged or cheated us in some way and we can't yet, forgive them. We get angry with ourselves for the mistakes we've made that we're not yet ready to forgive ourselves. When it comes to the suicide of a loved one, who wouldn't feel cheated and desperately angry at the person now gone whom they loved and trusted? Especially their child? Who wouldn't feel angry with themselves for the mistakes they made and missing all the signs of their loved one's impending death? Especially their child?

No one ever sees a suicide coming. It rocks every survivor to their core. Many people never recover from the loss. There's a lot to feel angry about and much to forgive. All of which takes time to process in grief.

If I were to be honest, I can admit I'm still a little angry with you, dear daughter, for choosing to die. For everything else that may have gone wrong that made you want to die, I'm angry with myself. I feel as though I'm to blame. While this may not be true, it's how I feel, and changing our feelings is one of the most difficult things to do.

Nobody likes to admit they are angry. It's one of the most negatively impacting emotions in pain and one we may deny feeling in grief. In my early bereavement, I was consumed by anger and regularly took it out on anyone or thing provoking me. Usually, we reserve taking out the worst of our anger on our closest loved ones. Except for your brother, I was angry at everyone. With myself. At life itself.

Through the years I learned that my anger was only about me. Nobody else. The degree to which I'd internalized it was because it was so painful to dig deep to see what I was really angry about. Part of this I had a fleeting sense was because I felt you had abandoned me. How could you? I honestly thought you knew I loved you more than life itself. Equal to your brother. That you could leave me in such a devastating way – leave all of us, was unthinkable and felt like the worst betrayal of all. But I didn't want to be angry with you. Ever. It was easier to push the anger away or just be angry with myself.

It wasn't until a decade later and I took the time to explore what all that I'd been emotionally struggling with for years had done to my body. Strangely, though I've always felt tenseness in my body since your death, it was only by attending regular therapy massage sessions that I wished I'd started years earlier, I began to realize just how stiff and unresponsive my body had become. I felt pain in areas I didn't know my body could hold pain. I am certain much of this was from the buried anger that I didn't want to admit I was feeling. If I wasn't blowing up there was nowhere for it to go but places inside my body. And there it's stayed.

I doubt I'm completely over anger. But I know I don't want to live as an angry person. I've suffered illness, headaches, sore throat, tummy aches and pain throughout my body. This isn't even addressing the physical symptoms from other pain and stress that have attacked my body from all the trauma triggers and unresolved complexities of grief over the years. Sounds awful, right?

Anger also comes from fear. And there's been plenty of that to go around in grief. Fear has ruled every other emotion I maybe could control (there's a difference between fear that is trauma based and fear that is pain based). When you died, I'm certain fear replaced the shock and with the fear, arose my anger, realizing I would have to live without you forever on this planet. I still remember being frightened beyond belief from the *second* I learned you had died. It's a moment I won't ever forget.

To not feel angry, I must let you go in whatever way I am holding you to me in fear. The biggest one that I may have failed you in some way that contributed to your choice to die.

If I knew then what I know now, I would warn newly bereaved parents to expect a turbulence of emotions from everyone grieving in the household that will disrupt their life in all areas as a result of everyone's anger. Everyone will be angry that their child died. Not just the parents. Siblings, extended family, their friends.

Anger can rip families apart for a time. Understanding that explosive emotions are mostly associated with earlier grief, they can feel assured that calm will prevail once again. Having said this, individuals have to be aware of their own anger and not fall into the trap of only wanting to blame others for theirs. Everyone says and does things in shock, trauma and grief that they will regret. Even when they don't know what else to do with their anger for that moment, the options are to apologize, retreat and explain what they are feeling that is causing them to react with anger.

In my situation, I found that my family always forgave me my outbursts. I was the more emotionally demonstrative of the three of us, though our son displayed plenty of anger in the first year after his sister's suicide. Suffering from chronic illness, disinterest, lethargy and anger, we eventually met with his teachers to explain the situation. We put a plan in place that everyone, including our son, felt comfortable with to ease the pressures he was feeling in his grief. Talking through his challenges and coming up with a plan for each one of them helped him recover from illness, feel less angry, and get through all the stages of his schooling and university. Our family has stuck together, though we've had several rocky patches. We continue to support each other the best we can, but ultimately how anybody chooses to be in their relationships is up to them.

None of us likes to admit being an angry person. Someone once pointed out to me in the first weeks of my bereavement how angry I was. I felt resentful and thought they were completely wrong. Maybe we don't like to admit to our anger because it makes us look weak and childish. Also, nobody wants to be around angry people. Anger is an effective emotion to keep people away.

I'd suggest that anger plays a central role in grief to safeguard the griever and give the illusion they are in control of their pain. Additionally, because many grievers do not understand how to express all of what they are feeling, getting angry at others is a common way to release some of these emotions. Getting angry with themselves may come out in different ways, none of which are healthy. Physically, and as examples, this may be through excessive use of alcohol, drugs, violence, risk behaviors. Internally, it will be any number of ways they beat themselves up emotionally.

I would tell the newly bereaved that being accountable for their anger will allow them to start managing it. It's incredibly freeing to feel angry and let those around know that you are upset and just need to get it out. To this day, certain things still trigger me where I can react explosively. Always a verbal outburst, it will be over as quick as it began.

My son became excellent at spotting my mood shifts and is able to defuse any potential conflict or calm me down just using humor. The most important change in my level of anger though has come from me just not wanting to be an angry person. Ever.

The newly bereaved should remember that they are not responsible for anyone else's anger. However, the more they are aware of their own anger, the more attuned they will be to the anger in those around them.

Insight about all of what they are feeling in grief will help them find the tools, support, therapy, and whatever else they need to steer themselves and their loved ones away from all conflict.

The worst type of anger in grief to contend with is silence. Anger that is buried simmers and stews until eventually, it does explode. It is good for grievers to remember that everyone in a family coping with the suicide of a child is dealing with the same shock, trauma and range of emotions, though perhaps on a different scale and in different ways. Every difficulty in grief makes it easy for the grieving parent to forget that their partner, children and other loved ones are experiencing pain from such a devastating loss, too. Having compassion for each other is critical to preserving and rebuilding these relationships stronger and better than before. They will be different by the very nature of the changed family dynamic. Loved ones get angry about this too.

I've learned that it's best never to assume what a loved one is going through. One thing is for sure. They will not be going through the same thing together at any one time. Grief doesn't work like that. I've always believed that grief is much the same for everyone, though our circumstances are different. If one was to strip away behaviors, actions, preferences and abilities, whatever is driving them is coming from the same family of emotions. There are only so many to go around. It is important to remember we are not that different from each other in grief.

Finally, I would share with the newly bereaved and those still struggling with anger, one of the first things they can do to get rid of anger is to decide for themselves how angry a person they want to be. Ultimately, anger only hurts the one who is angry. Using humor to deflect conflict, deciding to have a more positive outlook, remembering how deeply they love and care for those around them, understanding there is a solution for every problem can help them defuse their anger. They can take comfort knowing that every difficult stage of their grief will eventually pass as they heal.

Trust

O h, sweet daughter. My world came crashing down the instant I learned of your death. I can still recall the *exact* sensation that filled my body and took the life right out of me the instant I heard you were gone. In fact, the words "she is gone" can still haunt me at times.

After you died, I lost all trust in everyone and everything. Before this, my sense of well-being was based entirely on the love and support our family had for each other. Our family was my world. I can still recall how happy I felt from those things that make every parent feel good inside: pride in all of the family's accomplishments and relief that no harm had come to any of us. I didn't think too much about the tragedies that had befallen people, other than to feel a genuine sympathy and sadness for them when I'd heard what had happened to them or read about their stories in the news. I had zero experience with grief. In fact, I didn't think about death at all outside my metaphysical interest in the topic.

With my world instantly blown apart the second you left this planet, sweet girl, the ground beneath me seemed unsafe. I can still remember how wobbly I felt on my feet. I felt the earth would crack wide open and swallow me up whole at any moment.

I instantly lost my identity. One second I was a mom of two: you and your brother. The next, a mom of one. An only son. There was no more daughter. I was at a total loss as to who I was and what to do.

We have trust when we feel confident the outcome we are expecting will occur. Before you died, I trusted we all would have a good, long life. I was proud of the success our family enjoyed and expected it to continue. When you died, all of this instantly shattered. With my world crushed and all of my confidence gone, I couldn't see a future for those of us remaining. There was nothing to feel hopeful about.

In my early grief, I couldn't trust people to carry through with their word. Situations were not working out favorably for me. In fact, life was a living hell. I didn't trust in my abilities, much less those of others to see me through this horrific ordeal.

There was no relief in sight from the pain and problems weighing me down. The endless struggles were proof enough for me that life could not be trusted. It seemed as though I'd fallen down a rabbit hole so far, I'd never be able to find my way out. I wanted to die, too.

I had no understanding of the grief I was in or what I could expect. There was little information to guide me. I quickly discovered that grief is a never-ending grind. It's like a full-time job, but no one tells you that. They expect you to get over it. There are even time limits employers set instructing when their workers must return to work.

Grief is not this simple. In fact, when it comes to burying a child, grief is not simple at all. Every child's death is shocking and traumatic. The grief unpredictable. I've had discussions with health professionals about why it is a child's death feels like death for the parents too. Is it because our child has taken with them a very real part of our own DNA?

There is this feeling of lifelessness I've had since you died, sweet daughter, that has never gone away. Immediately after your death, I lost all interest in everything. I could not trust that anything would ever be right in my world again. Your death instantly taught me just how vulnerable we all are. That life itself could not be trusted.

I have contemplated trust a lot. I realize that trust must start with me. I've known this for years. Before your death, I placed an enormous amount of trust in my abilities and life itself. Since your death, it's been impossible to gauge. I have to wonder what it is I no longer trust about myself? Could it be related to this loss of my identity that has me searching still for something that will bring me meaning and give to me a better sense of self?

Knowing who we are is essential if we are to think about what we want and where we want to go. There is this spark of hope that drives us to feel certain that a bright and exciting future awaits us. If we don't know who we are or where we want to go, how can we possibly trust ourselves to get there? It's like digging around in the sand to find our castle.

I know that I don't want to define myself only as a bereaved mom. Yet, I still feel challenged to change this, at least in my private thoughts. In death, you remain an integral part of my living. All of what I do and think about is wrapped up in this one loss experience. Everything I did before no longer matters.

I believe that once I know who I am, I will be able to find my authentic place in the world again. But, just how easy this will be I'm not so sure. Nothing that I've done so far has felt quite right. In a way, I still feel like I'm grasping at loose straws, because I don't yet know with what or how to fill the part of me that died with you.

I can still remember the world I once lived in, where I knew what I was capable of and where I wanted to go. Today, living in a world much less populated by those who would truly understand me, it still feels remote and isolating. I sometimes struggle to believe I can be different or do more to fit in.

We connect with each other through the sharing of our common experiences and interests. Because nothing was the same for me after you died, darling girl, everything I identified with instantly left me. I felt rudderless, adrift in a sea of despair. While I no longer feel this same despair, there are still few people with whom I feel a connection or share similar interests and experiences. While not everyone I enjoy being around is bereaved, I know my general lack of trust in others is more about protecting my vulnerability and feeling that I can't be heard. I don't ever want to let myself get hurt again.

If I knew then what I know now, I would tell newly bereaved parents that it is natural to mistrust everything and everyone after losing their child. Child death is a shocking reminder of how suddenly one's life can change. With suicide, like every other sudden death, there is no time to prepare. No time to say goodbye. But different from other sudden death, with a suicide, there can never be a full understanding of what took our loved one from us. Losing young adults, teens and children to suicide remains incomprehensible to most of society. As parents, it makes us lose our faith in all that we once trusted.

I would tell them that while it will be natural to want to lean on those closest to them to help them in their worst pain, the complications from child loss are so complex that the people they think they can rely on, may not be the ones that can support them in their grief. Which makes it difficult to know who to trust. One small disappointment can lead to problems in relationships that sometimes can never be repaired. The need to blame others for their loss and the overwhelming resentment, anger, bitterness, jealousy, envy, judgment and even vengefulness they feel towards others can quickly arise from the need to protect themselves in pain. And, where these emotions exist, there is no trust.

A child's death rips every bereaved parent apart and leaves them feeling exposed and vulnerable. It can be hard to let the walls down. The need to protect themselves from further pain can force bereaved parents to shut people out who can't relate to the horror of their loss.

Trusting others requires that they let people into their world, even just a little. Trusting themselves will require a lot more than that. Not least, that they love themselves and feel compassion and forgiveness for all they believe they have done wrong. Not saving their child may rank high on the list of things to forgive. It can feel like a lot to ask they trust themselves to do better in any area of their life. To feel self-forgiveness, love and trust in themselves again takes time.

Trust also has a lot to do with the feelings of self-worth, and all they may be questioning about what they deserve after losing the one person they were entrusted to cherish and protect until the day they die. Their child. It takes time to sort these complex emotions out, too.

Self-Love

My darling daughter, right from the beginning of my grief, I met many bereaved parents that would not consider indulging themselves in any way, least of all self-love. Self-punishment ruled the day. While I had a natural inclination to nurture my physical self, it wasn't until years later I realized just how hard I had been on my emotional self. My difficult inner manager had been demanding more of me than I could handle. There was no caring or compassion for the me that felt responsible for any part I may have played in your death.

Self-love is the instinct we have to preserve our well-being at all costs. While some may think this vain, in the context of suffering, it is essential we find it within ourselves to love and feel compassion for who we are and all we have experienced.

The definition of love is to feel a profoundly tender or passionate affection for another person. Why then, is it so difficult and even feels wrong to love ourselves, when it is exactly the right thing to do?

Realizing much too late the extent to which I've punished myself for your death over the years has been both a blessing, but still more pain. The emotional toll has been excessive. And all because I've never quite been able to accept there wasn't more I could and should have done to save you.

I have blamed and tortured myself in heart and mind, thinking about all that could have been. Our lives as they should have been had I not been so blind to your suffering. Would you still be here if I had done just one thing differently?

Loving myself through all this pain has been impossible. Thinking about your suicide, there have been many things to consider that may have gone wrong to make you want to die. I've spent years thinking about what this may have been and how and when things changed. How much of it really was my fault? Should I have known better? Equally though, who expects their child to die? You up and dying on us was not something I ever considered.

For all those things I've thought of as failures in my life, not being able to protect you has been the biggest of them all. While it's been easy to see the lessons in every other one, your death has challenged me the most to feel love, forgiveness and compassion for myself for all I did before and have been through since you died. I hold myself responsible for your death.

Regardless of the fact that I've been told often enough I did the best I could with what I knew, this all seems rather cliché now. I still believe it was my responsibility to protect and save you, even though I had no clue from what. I feel I could have done a better job as your mom.

That I should have been more aware of your vulnerabilities. That maybe I pushed you to do things I should have understood weren't in your best interests. That I should have listened to you more, even though I thought I was listening. Whether or not this is irrational thinking on my part (everyone who knows me assures me I was a great mom), what matters most is what I believe.

I know instinctively that loving myself through all this self-reproach is right for me to do. It's time I start. And I want to. I really do. But, I'm wondering, what would I have to give up if I'm no longer going to make myself feel responsible for your death?

To love myself would suggest I must put my well-being above all malcontent I feel for myself and most importantly, my suffering.

Within this context, I know that loving me is not a selfish or incomprehensible thing to do. It would actually help me create that more fulfilled and happy life I've been saying I want.

When I think about the emotional damage done to countless parents from the death of their child and bereaved siblings from losing a brother or sister when they were young, I am reminded just how much love is needed to get ourselves through the pain. Every surviving loved one I've met where a younger family member died instantly robbed the whole family of the love and joy that they felt prior to the loss. As adults, every bereaved sibling I've ever met still feels haunted by the loss and drastic change within the family. They felt they were left further bereaved by the grief their parents never got over. Many even blame themselves in some way for their sibling's death.

After a child dies, it's important to remember that it's not just the lives of parents that are ruined. Every relationship in the family changes. Everybody's heart gets broken. Everyone feels challenged in some way to fully love themselves and others as the years go by.

I wonder also if by denying myself the love I need it's a reflection of what I can or can't yet feel for others. When we love ourselves, it's natural to extend this love to those around us. Sometimes, I think that maybe I prefer to keep myself apart from people so I can continue to suffer alone. Sometimes, it just feels safer this way.

While I am grateful that my heart did not shut down completely where your brother is concerned; he reflects that spark of love and joy within me that has never died completely, in every other sense I've struggled to feel love the way I once did. Not only for myself, but others too.

While I know that the healing of anyone else is not my responsibility, I do think how we feel about ourselves can be felt by those around us. Whether love for one's self is enough to influence others to change their minds about how they feel about themselves,

I have no idea. I just think my own loved ones would be pleasantly surprised if one day, the harshness I've long felt towards myself wasn't quite so obvious to see.

If I knew then what I know now, I would remind newly bereaved parents that self-love is difficult enough for anyone to feel without the complications of tragedy and grief thrown into the mix. Factoring in child loss, I would tell them to expect that finding the will to love themselves again will probably be one of the hardest and most long-suffering parts of their grief. Despite the self-criticism and loathing they are sure to feel for a long time, staying mindful of how important self-love is in general to help us grow and heal, is a huge step in the right direction to help them through all of their healing in grief. It will soften the edges of their heart, little by little.

Early in grief, it's likely it will not be possible for the newly bereaved to think too much about anything that benefits themselves. Grieving parents can expect to struggle for years with all types of self-defeating emotions. I've never been one to believe it's better to try and run from pain, though it's fair to say fifteen years in grief has given me the hindsight to know it takes a long time to even feel ready to more fully understand our grief. The emotional pain is incredibly difficult to dive into, let alone try to comprehend. It takes courage and time. Lots of time.

While it could be that the more positive we felt about ourselves before the loss of our child may help us regain a positive sense of self more quickly in our grief, and perhaps lead us to enjoy a more fulfilling life, I'm not convinced a quicker recovery may be based on personality type or former positive sense of self, alone. I enjoyed a good sense of self and abundant life in every sense of the word before my daughter died. I have an abundant life now. However, the level of enjoyment I can feel is not what it once was.

The weight a bereaved parent can carry feeling responsible for the suicide of their child can be heavy and long-lasting. In fact, I'm certain it's the same for every bereaved parent who feels this same responsibility, regardless of how their child died. Setting aside traumatic effects or the symptoms of Post-Traumatic Stress Disorder that negatively impact our emotions and thought processes differently, newly bereaved parents can expect to feel a heightened sense of responsibility for their child's suicide, when in fact, it isn't their fault at all. It's important to know the difference between thoughts and feelings that are natural to feel in grief and the more harmful and self-demoralizing ones triggered by trauma.

Having struggled for years with this feeling of excess burden of responsibility that has resulted in my degraded sense of self, my goal now is to let this struggle go. Intellectually, I understand there's a whole lot I don't understand about my daughter or what made her choose to die. But I do know it wasn't only about one thing. Intellectually, I'm not certain it had anything to do with me at all. But speaking as a mom and from my heart, I'm not yet ready to consider this any further.

I would encourage newly bereaved parents to remember that the caring of their mind, body, spirit and soul is essential to help them heal throughout their grief. Forgiving what they can of their former selves will help them feel love and tenderness for themselves again too, one day.

Joy

Joy is defined as happiness that comes from a deep feeling of contentment. Our pleasure and delight are triggered by someone or something that feels exceptionally good or satisfying to us. When I think about my chase for joy all these years since you died, sweet daughter, apart from your brother's efforts and successes (he truly does bring me great joy), being able to point to what I've done or a situation that has brought me the contentment I seek, I keep coming up empty-handed. What is there to feel joyous about? I'm not even sure I'll ever be able to feel this emotion again.

Sure, I have experienced fleeting bursts of happiness when something great has happened for anyone in our family. But feeling happy is not a state I can maintain for long. I want to feel joy and contentment from all that I am doing and surrounded by most of the time. I can't think why this wouldn't be possible.

There is empty space in my heart that when you were here was filled with joy. For years, I've been on a search to find a way to fill it up again. Memories of happier times don't do it. In fact, most of them are still too hard for me to think about: all of them a glaring reminder of all that we once had. This rearview perspective always prominently displays the one piece missing. You.

I've thought a lot about what could bring me joy again. I know the feeling must come from within. I like to think that when we do feel joy, it can help us through anything. I'm certain it would help me view my current circumstances and the future differently.

I also think that one's ability to express pure joy for life comes from feeling grateful for all of our experiences; both good and bad. Being able to appreciate our hardest times and the worst of our suffering helps us grow. It gives us wisdom.

Every former difficulty I've learned to appreciate as one of a series of never-ending life events that help us to evolve. The more we get the lessons, the less intense they are and the fewer they become. We move on.

While I recognize my growth and wisdom gained from every previous difficulty, all that I've struggled with after losing you, my child, has left me a long way still from appreciating all the lessons. I'm not so sure they've all been worth the suffering. None of the progress I've made (healing) has brought me the contentment or joy I'd otherwise feel from knowing I can now move on. In fact, I feel stuck. Uncertain where to go.

While I can acknowledge the peace there is in accepting there are lessons in every difficulty, I have yet to even want to acknowledge the same is true from this experience of losing you. I'd rather have you here than lessons any day.

When I think about serving as a means of joy (helping people is what I mostly do), it does have a way of lifting me out of my pain. However, this is different from the joy I had and want to feel again from those around me. My family. Intact.

I know that searching for lasting joy from anything external will not help me fill this inner void. Anyone who claims this to be true, I believe will find that at the end of the day, they are still left with the same amount of pain, though buried a little deeper.

While I can believe that there are people who have suffered who have found their inner joy again from something or someone,

I still have not. Though I can feel snippets of pleasure from the love I feel for my family and passion work I do, neither has quite filled the empty space that you once did.

Maybe joy will come to me again from just deciding to have a more positive outlook on life. In believing that I can feel fulfilled just by acquiring an appreciation for all I've learned and can admit has been worthwhile. The challenge comes in letting go of all the thoughts that still torment me.

If I knew then what I know now, I would tell all parents grieving unbearable loss not to expect to feel joy from anything for quite a while. But when it happens, to take it as a good sign.

The return of joy will come to them in many ways beginning in early grief. In these early weeks and months and even first few years, it is common to feel a deadening within. As though all five senses have been dulled or completely flattened. Parents new to grief may read in books or hear from other bereaved parents in a support group how they felt their senses immediately dull right after losing their child. How their appreciation for everything they liked or loved before instantly left them.

I can still recall the moment in my early grief that I could see the actual colors of the flowers in my garden once again. Before this, for months and maybe an entire year, I could barely look at what had been a major source of joy for me. Before my daughter died, from spring to fall, I'd wander through the beds and with delight, spot the growth and drink in every scent and color from the various flowers and shrubs. It was a meditation of sorts.

When my daughter died, I couldn't feel an appreciation for anything I had before. I saw everything as if I were looking through gauze. I was saddened by the fact that all I'd cared about before my daughter's death represented nothing but heartache in my grief.

The realization this one day that I could see color, standing on my deck looking at my flowers, came with just the tiniest spark of appreciation I once felt for their beauty. While the joy didn't stay, what's important is that I remembered the feeling of the spark. Eventually, I had others more frequently that mimicked it.

While none of these joyful moments of my early grief morphed into my lasting joy for life, they anchored me early on to what joy had remained in me. A joy that was its own sort of hope.

I would caution all newly bereaved parents that this time in grief they can't feel joy or have an appreciation for anything is one that can't be controlled. No one can force themselves to feel something that they can't. However, they can trust that one day they will be able to feel something more than only pain. Every positive emotion they eventually will express will come to them in its own way and time.

Until then, they should avoid punishing themselves mentally and emotionally for not being able to feel the things they can't. It's normal to *not* feel happy in grief. Pushing themselves to feel and behave differently from what they actually do is a recipe for disaster. It creates nothing but conflict. There are ways to live in pain without being offensive to others. Requesting privacy, understanding, compassion and assistance, and giving the same to loved ones who need this too, is healing in itself.

I would encourage all grieving parents that in the absence of feeling joy in their life, they first work on trying to feel gratitude for any of their difficult experiences that they can. This will help them develop an appreciation for all the efforts they have made prior to their child dying, and certainly in trying to survive their child's suicide.

They can feel confident that their journey to heal is their own. It will take the course it's meant to in accordance with their own situation, beliefs, abilities and outlook. It's helpful to think about all the experiences shared by other bereaved parents, myself included, as information that may guide them to reflect on their own experience and as a support to help them get through their own unique challenges.

Ambition

Ambition is described as the earnest desire for achievement and the willingness it takes to strive for its attainment. This may relate to power, wealth, honor or fame in "normal" life. For those of us hit with adversity and struggling, there are many more things that require ambition just to survive, never mind pursue a fulfilling life.

When I think about ambition beyond only my survival, which is how I lived for many years in grief, any desire I've felt to want more for my life has always pushed and pulled at me in various ways. Mostly, I have felt this swinging of emotions when I consider all that it would take, to not only pursue, but maintain a busier and more fulfilling life. A life filled with all those things that many people take for granted who are not challenged by adversity.

When I think about my work, to always want to be and do more requires constant planning, creating, meeting and networking. On the personal side, being more involved means more socializing, entertaining, making an effort to see old friends and make new ones. Getting involved in my community. I get tired just thinking about it, though I do believe all these things would give me a more rounded life. It's how I used to live.

To this point in my grief, I've worked hard to contribute to the greater good. At least, with respect to changing how we think about grief. But things get mentally challenging for me when I start to consider all it would really take for me to take things to another level, and the drive I would need to stay afloat if I even got further ahead. It feels especially stressful when I observe the abilities of others on their rise to the top of their game (whatever this is) and the drive they must have to do whatever it takes to stay there. I'm not sure I have it in me anymore.

It's not that I'm comparing myself to anyone, but with every success I see someone achieve, it mentally pushes me to do more. At the same time, I feel weighed down by my limitations that often prohibit me from doing things. Coping with this new reality of mine, I get frustrated thinking about what I really can do. I've never been one to sit around and do nothing. It's just that I now have a body that can't keep up with my busy mind.

There is another struggle with ambition against this backdrop of adversity. I can't really see much of what I've already done as major accomplishments or associate these achievements with ambition. I seem to have this need to just keep pushing myself to do more. To be better, but for what reason I'm not sure. Strange that I would feel this given the number of times I've reminded others to be wary of the same thing in their grief. Perhaps I am trying to make up for some kind of deficiency in my character that I believe only ambition would fix.

As I contemplate further how necessary ambition is to achieving success, I sense a big challenge ahead of me if I truly want to experience a more well-rounded life. Grief has hampered my ability to feel much of anything. I don't get excited very often, nor do I have the energy to vigorously pursue goals. As a result, much of what I desire doesn't get beyond being a great idea in my head. My darling daughter, everything feels so much harder since you died.

While I won't get into the semantics of success, I find myself thinking back to early grief and the ambition it took for me just to get out of bed. To move. To put a smile on my face to greet your brother every morning. To stay strong. All of these achievements many people may not even think of as requiring ambition. But in grief, they do.

It is true that the longer we have been in grief the more we naturally start to fill up our lives again with people, pursuits and things. As did I. All of which requires ambition. And while I don't mean to sound entirely defeated by life, because I do enjoy a lot, in thinking further about the struggle I feel to always be and do more, I wonder if this isn't the result of my feeling I have failed to fulfill the one desire I cannot ever fill. That is, to see and feel my life again as it was before you died.

If I knew then what I know now, I would tell newly bereaved parents that there is a difference between surviving their child's death and living with their child's death. The two are uniquely different. The first is experienced in earlier grief and will demand from them the will to carry on. Mostly, they will find this by forcing themselves to do what is required or expected of them to meet their obligations within their family, work and social environments, for however long.

It will take enormous courage and strength for any new bereaved parent just to sort out what they need to do as an individual and as a family to survive. Coping with relationship and other conflicts, health issues, financial challenges, job loss or change, tending to their surviving children, and any number of other stressors can create many situations where they will rely only on their gut reaction to get them through. Bereaved parents must stay alert to how they are feeling about anything they may be trying to force themselves to do too early in their grief.

Eventually, bereaved parents graduate from surviving in grief to living with their child's loss once they have a better understanding of their grief and how they have changed. While it takes a certain ambition to only survive, ambition is generally thought of as the desire we have to achieve something specific. The first year or two in grief is not the time for the newly bereaved to try and figure out all of what they want and need. There will be many changes.

Looking ahead, I'd tell newly bereaved parents that when they do feel more adjusted to their grief, they can still expect to be hit with surges of emotions brought on by challenges and triggers. Grief is unpredictable. The same emotions felt in the early months and years can quickly be triggered by events, memories and other reminders of their child that can take them right back to the trauma they experienced the day that child died. Because of the complexities of grief from child loss and this unpredictability, and regardless that they likely will have established a new rhythm for their life, triggers can set them back. Each step forward will seem lost. Experiencing setbacks enough times can make any bereaved parent think they'll never get past a certain point in their grief, which is frustrating.

When dealing with complicated grief, it can be hard to see the future, let alone drum up ambition to create a better life. This may partly explain why, as bereaved parents, we feel like we are always just trying to survive our child's death and aren't really living at all.

There is zero understanding of the bereaved parent's experience beyond what bereaved parents feel and experience themselves. The challenge for anyone to fit into mainstream society is driven largely by what we do. Not who we are. For bereaved parents, the desire to fit in and ambition to succeed is difficult at best when we already feel so lost.

Countless bereaved parents have had to abandon or change jobs, careers, goals and ideas after losing their child. It may be more realistic and even comforting to think about ambition as the drive that we may have to move ourselves to be or do just a little more than what we already can at any stage throughout our grief.

I remember in my first year of grief meeting parents that were years into their bereavement. At the time, I wanted to skip all of my journey and land myself right where they were. I was convinced they had mastered what it took to do more than just survive their child's death. I wanted to know how they did it (by the way, none were claiming they had).

Having reached this place myself, I can honestly say that grieving the loss of a child doesn't get easier. I've since discovered that every bereaved parent says the same thing. About ten years into my grief, I realized with some despair that I may never recover completely from the pain of losing my daughter. Thinking this way made me feel like I was giving into something I didn't want to believe. Yet, the moment was pivotal in that it changed the way I thought about my grief going forward. Since then, I've made a serious effort to put a stop to the demands I've been placing on myself and instead, find a way to create the balance I need in my life, yet still do what I want to do.

I would say to the newly bereaved, whether they have a demanding personality or not; they are overly ambitious or not; to always be kind to themselves in their grief. Always be respectful of who they are becoming in their grief. And always remember that the hurdles they must jump to get where they are going will feel different from who they were before their bereavement.

Identity

Identity is the state of remaining the same under varying aspects or conditions. We gain a sense of self or our identity, from our unique character traits, beliefs, and predominant mental and emotional state that shapes our outlook on life. Unless something takes us drastically off course, our basic nature and the way we handle our ups and downs doesn't change.

Your death, sweet daughter, rocked me to my core. It took my identity with it. With everything crashing all around me, I instantly lost my sense of self. I was confused by who I now was as a wife, mother, sister and daughter. The circumstances I found myself in sent me tumbling down a rabbit hole with no end in sight. The darkness all around me seemed like it would last an eternity.

Until then, I'd had a pretty good idea of who I was and how to get things done. Others saw me as strong and capable. They came to me with their problems. Because I had always been so independent, it was difficult for me to ask for help. I'd always dealt with challenges on my own. Grief was something new and unfamiliar. I no longer felt like I was in control of anything.

With everything I'd ever known collapsing, I no longer felt I could trust the world, much less speculate about my proper place in it. To that point, though I'd had many interests and had done interesting things, my life was centered on being a mom and keeping my family safe.

With the instant evaporation of all I had believed in, my spirit crushed and my outlook grim, I floundered like a newborn pup trying to find my way in this new world, while trying to stay sturdy on my feet. There was nobody to guide or help me make sense of what I was going through in the aftermath of your death. I didn't know how I was going to survive. Thinking about the endless years ahead, my life seemed bleak. I was at a complete loss as to how to be, what to do or where to go.

Though at first, I didn't attribute this major change in me to a loss of my identity, I've thought about identity a lot since gaining a better understanding of my grief. I hate to admit that today, I still feel confused about whether to call myself a mom of one or two, or whether to identify myself as bereaved or not. None and all of it makes sense. I feel pressured by the situations I am in and whoever I am speaking with to respond a certain way. Sadly, to this day, and the same as when you were first gone, no one wants to hear too much about you or me in my bereavement.

The only times I've ever felt safe enough to share with others who I really am, which is a bereaved mom of two with one of you deceased, is when I am with other bereaved parents. This constant silencing of my voice has not been easy to live with all these years. It feels like I am hiding myself from others. Like I am not being truthful with myself.

We cling to our identity to fit in and connect with others. Before your death, sweet daughter, I was a happy mom of two. Our family was the cornerstone of my life, centered around the enjoyment that all this entails. I hung out with people who felt the same way. Your death stole from me the ability to dream about the future I could see for all of us.

As my daughter, I was so proud of who you were and all that you could do. You were smart and beautiful. My sidekick in every way that only a daughter can be. I had so much hope that all the stresses of your youth would one day all be gone. That you would find yourself. Instead, I am bereaved and still unable to reconcile myself to my misfortune.

I am so different now. All those traits I once identified within me, I no longer do. I used to laugh more. Tackle life with gusto. Now, I'm not sure who I can or want to be. I've been trying for years to understand who I've become.

If I knew then what I know now, I would tell newly bereaved parents not to expect a return to their former self. Years into my grief, I can honestly say that every bereaved parent I've ever met has never regained a sense of who they were before their loss.

When as a newly bereaved parent you find you are very different, it can feel disheartening and even scary to realize you no longer are the same or have an appreciation for what you once did. Letting parts of yourself go can be difficult. Sometimes, it felt like I was losing my daughter all over again when I realized I would never be able to return to former interests.

I used to play piano right up until my daughter died. My mom was an accomplished pianist and gave me lessons. This love for music had bonded us since I was a child. After my daughter's death, I couldn't listen to music, much less lay my fingers on the piano keys. Only a month before her death, my daughter had attended a recital at which I had performed. I was so excited that she was there and proud of me. After her death, playing the piano became too painful a reminder of our life that was now gone.

The changes in me impacted all of my relationships in addition to causing me to question everything I knew and had believed in. My daughter's suicide robbed me of myself. As a bereaved parent, while I am certain I'm not alone in feeling this loss of self even years into my grief, it is important that those new to child loss consider that the loss of what they had previously identified with can make it challenging for them going back into the "normal" world. Trying to figure out their needs when they don't know who they are, and trying to manage the expectations of others, can be difficult.

The loss of identity can throw anyone off course. In terms of grief from child loss, I'd suggest it may be partially responsible for any number of mental health issues that can arise including depression, isolating behavior and even to some degree, dissociative behavior. Where there is concern, bereaved parents may want to seek therapy to learn more about at-risk issues related specifically to identity loss. Working with a professional may help them regain a better sense of self more quickly than being left to flounder on their own, desperately trying to understand what's happened to them.

I still like to think it's possible to change who we have become in our bereavement as parents, though I don't think this is a quick or simple process. While we may feel better about ourselves at various times in our grief, I believe there is a predominant way in which we view ourselves after the suicide of our child. For example, I've had a poorer sense of self with all the blame, regret and doubt I've struggled with over the years, thinking about any part I may have played in my daughter's choice to die. Additionally, not being comfortable identifying myself as a bereaved parent or a mom of two in the "normal" world has further complicated how and what I think of myself.

Certainly, I do think that what we believe influences how we think about ourselves. In my heart I know I am and always will be a mom of two. But my confidence in sharing this truth gets shaky when I think about having to explain to others that one of my children is deceased, whenever the situation arises. Which it almost always does whenever parents start talking about their children.

It's important for newly bereaved parents to know that their effort to regain a sense of self can get confusing when they no longer recognize any of their former traits. This can leave them feeling uncertain about who they now are. Also, it's likely that their former predominant mental and emotional state has been so drastically altered that their ability to believe in themselves in a way they might imagine may be difficult, even after many years. It's natural to lose confidence in grief after child loss. Feeling unsure about who they are, any bereaved parent, no matter how long they've been in grief, can have considerable trouble fitting in and connecting with others.

It also may be that many bereaved parents discover much sooner in grief who they don't want to become before knowing who they do want to be or what they want. I knew for certain from the first weeks of my bereavement that I didn't want to stare back at sad and vacant eyes forever that were the reflection of how dead I felt inside. I also didn't want to be defined only by this one tragic loss. My life had been filled with so much more. Most importantly, I didn't want to deprive my son of all I knew I could be again. I didn't want him to feel like he had lost his mom, too.

As a result of this, I have made a solid effort over the years to heal. To regain a sense of who I am. I really do believe this will occur when I finally can accept that I couldn't have changed a thing with regard to my daughter's death, no matter how much I've beaten myself up over the years believing that I could. I've reached a point now, despite not knowing whether this is true or not, that maybe what I think matters more than the truth itself. At least, with regard to ending all my struggle related to this one issue.

I used to trust that everything happens in life the way and when it's meant to. My daughter's suicide ripped this belief from me and made me question everything. As I came to once again believe this to be true for all things in my life, the one exception has been my daughter's death. Nothing else has challenged me as much to change what I believe.

Changing beliefs isn't easy for anyone. But for bereaved parents, I have concluded that often there may be no other way to help us get through some of the tougher parts of grief than by changing what we believe. I have no doubt that those new to parent bereavement will eventually recognize within themselves a spark of who they used to be (it took a few years, but I can't deny some of the old me still exists). But, where loss of such magnitude causes us to lose our overall sense of self, I wonder too, if there isn't the opportunity that will allow us to become who we were ultimately meant to be on this planet as a result of such suffering.

It is seriously doubtful I would have evolved into part of who I am today without having experienced this loss. In many ways, I am a better version of the old me. Perhaps accepting this would help me reinvent myself further and in a way that I could feel proud of once again.

Finally, I would tell any bereaved parent struggling with who they are after suffering such a loss to remember that it takes time to recover from being rocked to their core. Equally though, they can trust that in choosing to evolve from the lessons they can take from their grief, they can choose to be more than who they are today.

Limitations

Not until I was in my eleventh year of mourning for you, sweet daughter, did I realize the impact of the limitations I had been living with for years that had been placed on me the moment I heard of your passing. Though I didn't understand the cause of my debilitation until well into my grief, in the beginning of my bereavement I was a complete wreck and didn't know what was happening to me. As the years passed, I ignored the physical exhaustion and played down those things that were placing enormous pressure on me emotionally, mentally and physically. I thought it was my job to fix everything. I did what was required of me.

In looking back, I realize now that the limitations we experience from grief, apart from not being well understood, may not always feel the same. They can change over time and vary in grievers. Because we don't view grief as debilitating, and because one way or another all bereaved parents will turn into someone they can no longer recognize, the grief is always confusing; the pain terrifying at times.

For professionals trying to support bereaved parents, the lack of awareness about debilitating grief related to child loss makes the seriousness of the emotional, physical and mental suffering hard to understand and treat. For loved ones, it can make the return to healthy communication and intimacy difficult if not impossible, which leads to its own set of problems. It can alter other types of relationships in ways where sometimes, the damage from misunderstandings can never be repaired. Understanding how one is experiencing limitations in grief can be hard. Bereaved parents may feel a variety of effects that can quickly become permanently debilitating such as: a slowing down due to lack of energy, lack of motivation, the inability to focus, think clearly or in detail, mental, emotional and physical fatigue. The impact from trauma and stress can cause a variety of physical health problems, where the bereaved parent is either making repeated visits to the doctor for symptoms that can't be diagnosed, or they suffer in silence without understanding what is happening to them. They may try to rationalize or dismiss their symptoms as imaginary. They likely will not attribute them to grief.

When medical professionals can't diagnose or identify a cause for a health issue (grieving parents may not even mention their grief from child loss to their doctor), it's not possible for them to benefit from the right treatment. Without treatment, the effects of emotional distress from their grief can pose serious health risks to the bereaved that only worsen over time. Which is precisely what led to my eventual collapse after ten years.

Bereaved parents put considerable pressure on themselves to not be who they really are in their grief. Because of this they may refrain from seeing their doctor or discussing their grief with medical professionals if they even do relate physical ill-health to grief. As a result of the silence around child loss and grief, and the stigma of suicide, bereaved parents risk developing a range of health problems that can become permanently debilitating in some way due to the underlying emotional distress that their mind and body is continuously battling (I found this out the hard way).

Because grief from child loss requires a unique approach to support and treatment that I certainly never found, I struggled for years with chronic ill-health that I did not at first associate with my grief. I pushed through the pain and fatigue, did what was expected and needed of me and ignored everything else. While I certainly recognized early on I no longer had the ability to perform mentally or keep up physically the way I had before my bereavement, it wasn't until I was forced into a work disability ten years into my grief that I understood it was survival instinct alone that had been pushing me to keep going.

My darling girl, looking back it is still hard for me to really comprehend the mental and emotional damage your death has caused. Sometimes I still feel like an emotional mess. While I take full responsibility for how I'm experiencing my life (I'd never blame you for what has happened to me), I still feel it's important to acknowledge the damage done. This pressure we feel in society to get on with life and not talk about our loss is unthinkable. Imagine, me or any other parent having to stay silent about their child. For some of us it's been years. I still feel angry about this.

For years before my disability and in an effort to fit in and do what was required, I ignored my body screaming at me to slow down. Even though I knew something wasn't right, I needed it to finally give out to force me into change. At the beginning of my disability, I was afraid. I had always resisted the idea of looking weak in my grief. Now, here I was in total collapse. While I didn't really know what was wrong with me, I knew I wasn't functioning well. Additionally, I felt I had to fight any stigma I may face knowing it wasn't just physical limitations that were causing me to no longer function. I knew I was dealing with mental ones as well, though I hadn't yet connected these to my emotional trauma.

In truth, I didn't experience stigma from others with respect to looking after my mental health. Mostly, I discovered I was fighting with me, feeling I'd let myself down. Who of us wants to admit our weaknesses, least of all to ourselves? Even today, thinking about myself in terms of having limitations makes me wonder if I'm being too self-centered in my grief or over-reacting to whatever problems I should have dealt with long ago.

It's because of thoughts like these (irrational) and society not geared toward adequately supporting bereaved parents, I was uncertain at the start of my disability whether I would be able to find the help I needed. With everything I have undergone in my efforts to recover from losing you, sweet girl, I've found that people of all types and professions, unless they've shared the experience, can't imagine losing a child. For parents of living children, talking about child loss makes them feel fearful that the same thing could happen to them. The difficulty society has in general understanding grieving parents, even those who have the best intentions to help, can be put at a distinct disadvantage in terms of how much any bereaved parent can trust sharing their innermost thoughts with anyone who can't relate to their struggles.

I found speaking to medical professionals about limitations I didn't really understand made me feel the same way I felt in earlier grief talking to them about trauma. As though I shouldn't have limitations because they didn't arise from a more common experience that people aren't afraid to talk about. How do you explain to others the destruction of your spirit and soul; your mind and heart, that you barely understand yourself?

My sweet daughter, do you remember the strong, courageous woman I once was? After your death, I never wanted to be seen by anyone as weak or vulnerable. I resisted whatever was pulling me down and attempted to soldier on as some version of the former me.

When you died, to feel so broken so suddenly was shocking. In those earlier years in grief, whatever strength I found prevented me from asking others for help. The limitations that were always there that forced me to eventually get help, also helped me get honest with myself about all of me in my bereavement. They taught me that what I needed to achieve I couldn't do alone. This helped me put a team in place to get me to the next stage of my healing.

It took three years for me to understand my limitations and another two to learn how to manage them. I ultimately found it is essential I strive to always maintain a well-balanced life. To not put pressure on myself to be more than who I can be at any one time. To not compare myself to others.

I know. I'm starting to sound like a broken record throughout these pages. This idea of striving to be more than who we are in grief that is at the core of so many of the lessons.

If I knew then what I know now, I would tell newly bereaved parents to be aware of any limitations they may experience in mind and body that are the result of the havoc grief can inflict upon them. While they may not yet know the limitations they could struggle with, it is unlikely they will survive their child's suicide without feeling the impact of some changes that could be permanent. This may be a loss of energy. A noticeable slowing down. Mental strain. A loss of interest in former hobbies and social activities. Loss of focus. Limited attention span. The inability to handle the same responsibility they did before their bereavement. People, places and things can surprisingly annoy them. The list is endless. It is important they pay attention to anything that feels challenging or out of character to who they once were and make changes to their life accordingly.

In many ways, once they are understood, limitations can be viewed as an opportunity for bereaved parents to assess their specific needs. Whether these can be met immediately or must wait, with knowledge comes foresight. With foresight comes choice. And with choice, comes healing.

Understanding the true extent of the assault on one's mind and body in grief should not be underestimated. Knowing what they are going through can help new and even more experienced bereaved parents set themselves on a path that continuously supports their healing. While not all changes from growing awareness can or should be made too early or quickly in grief, understanding one's needs at all times is half the battle in triumphing over the challenges that healing in any amount presents after child loss.

I don't think I'm alone in acknowledging how hard I've been on myself over the years after the suicide of my daughter. I suspect most, if not all bereaved parents of a child who has chosen to die, beat themselves up regularly from the guilt, blame and shame they feel knowing their child didn't want to live. That is a LOT to survive.

I'd suspect anyone who hasn't suffered the same fate would think it's normal for people to struggle with certain mental and physical limitations after being emotionally knocked around after the death of one's child. I eventually gave in to the idea that it isn't a sign of weakness or failure on my part or that of any bereaved parent who has to slow down, drop out and continually be on the search for those things that can bring comfort, respite, freedom and peace from all that torments us.

Despite the obvious frustrations that limitations impose on our abilities, interests, health and maybe even recovery, it doesn't mean we can't still pursue what we want. It may just be more realistic to accept that the results we get might be a little different from what we would have hoped for prior to our bereavement. We may have to modify our goals or shift the goal posts more often. We may have to switch ideas about what we want. We may have to completely redefine what success means to us.

While this may not sound too different for those not struggling with complicated grief, the difference is the degree to which as bereaved parents, we continually beat ourselves up, isolate, and feel impacted by the trauma and emotional distress after losing our child. What we can do to ourselves trying to survive the suicide of our child can make the mental and emotional suffering feel extreme. Sometimes, it seems like we have no chance at all to even get ourselves past the gate in anything we may want to accomplish, so damaged can we feel. Limitations that may well be a part of all grief related to child loss, no matter how our child has died, can teach us to become the person we are meant to be in our bereavement.

I've often thought about life chapters and how when they are done, they're done. Admittedly, it's been difficult to view my life as having had a chapter with my daughter in it and now another with her gone. In reality though, this is the truth.

Thinking about my own end and how I'll come to view all of my life since my daughter's death, I find it hard to imagine what my final thoughts will be. Will I have achieved that state I say I want, accepting all things were meant to be? Will there still be pain? Regret? Will I have missed more because of who I am today? Or will I have lived truly well exactly because of who I am today?

Limitations give us the chance to slow down and take stock of what's important moving forward. Of what we feel ready to let go of. Of what we need and want to change.

Change

Oh, sweet girl, what didn't change after you died? Today, years later, whenever I am in the company of other bereaved parents, I see they wear their changes on their face the same as me.

Where do I begin? If I were only to grieve those things that immediately upon your death created irrevocable and horrific change for all of us, and the many situations I've endured since then that have challenged me to carry on, it wouldn't be fair to not acknowledge as well, those things that have changed me for the better. Yet, I don't seem to reflect on these as much as I should. Perhaps if I did, they would help me release you so that I can carry on in my world more peacefully. Easier said than done.

Anyone suffering loss is irrevocably changed by the very nature that relationship is no more. In this alone, there are many things to contemplate. Not least, the opportunities for growth and awareness that are heaped upon the bereaved. While the reason for and the manner of death of anyone may well determine the types of lessons for survivors, losing a child to suicide presents many opportunities for growth that I'm sure many grieving parents can do without. The trouble with lessons is that because they are so personal, they can be hard to figure out and harder still to accept when we do. All of which makes change, as the number one certainty after loss, difficult to predict and manage once it's upon us because we often don't know what we need in grief.

Change requires us to make decisions. Anything that feels like it is no longer working or is causing us pain under normal circumstances in life, at some point has to be addressed. The only other option is that we allow ourselves to exist in some form of self-denial or even self-destruction to try and avoid the inevitable. Which is change, even when we don't yet know what it will bring. It's no different in grief.

For the first several years in my grief, I felt forced into many changes just to survive. I reacted to every challenge from gut instinct alone in an effort to do whatever I had to do to make the problem go away. Whether this was to help meet recurring financial demands, or repair all of my relationships that had seriously fallen apart, every opportunity I believed would help solve the immediate problem was a bumbling attempt on my part to fix everything in my own and the family's shattered life that I alone felt responsible to fix. I felt pounded by problems at every turn and was existing only to put out the fires. Which did nothing to help me find any of the healing I desperately longed for and needed.

While to be sure there were several wonderful opportunities that came my way and I achieved a number of successes during this period, if you see your life as a problem, it's a problem. It's called surviving. When we are only surviving, we aren't responding to life or creating outcomes by our own design. We are reacting in fear and panic to whatever challenge comes our way, hoping like heck we won't be hit twice with the same potential devastation as the original one. The death of our child.

After a decade of surviving, my increasing awareness of the consequences of only reacting to every unwanted situation in my grief helped me find the courage to start thinking more seriously about what I needed and wanted, and trust that every decision I made from thoughtful consideration, would take me one step closer to creating the changes in my life that would continuously support my healing. Since then, I've never looked back. All of my decisions have been leading me right where I want to go, in small steps and as I feel ready to embrace more in my life.

Massive change is inevitable in grief related to child loss. While I once believed the focus should be on the healing outcome itself, I now think about healing as the process we go through to recognize what we need throughout all stages of our grief. It is in this recognition that ideas can form. Courage is born and chances are taken.

While life does get confusing as we become ready to confront more of our pain and sort out more of what we need, maintaining inner calm, remaining open to growing awareness, and knowing when to reach out for help, with the proper support and tools we can be safely guided through all our changes. We can't heal without change. But, trying to coordinate healing with others because we are afraid to find ourselves alone in our healing, won't work. What we need in grief and healing is unique to every individual. Which is one reason that family grief is so complicated.

It's not always easy finding the right resources in grief, especially early on when you don't have a clue what you are doing: for example, finding books that are helpful and feel comforting. The right support group to attend. The right therapist who is trained in understanding and treating the problems of grief related to child loss. Having a sensitive employer willing to grant work accommodations. The right people to support the family's needs (and the list goes on); any changes bereaved parents must make, have to come from them alone. No one will do it for them.

I still remember feeling such dismay when I realized I had to find whatever support I needed alone. This included help for the family. No one rushed in to offer assistance or guide us where to go for various kinds of help. I later came to understand this is partly because nobody really understands grief from child loss except the grievers themselves. Also, people didn't want to intrude in my life.

I felt enormous pressure trying to find the right type of support that would ensure all of the family would be okay, sweet daughter. That meant as individuals, a couple and a family with a surviving child. In fact, ensuring our family's survival was more important to me than healing myself. Caring for your brother and responding to the demands of family and work, I felt overwhelmed. Learning to appreciate and create change as something for my own benefit took me a long time.

Though I've experienced the one step forward ten steps backward effect that is unique to certain types of recovery more times than I can count, I haven't let it get me down. I have long remembered that change is the one constant you can count on in grief. It's just that now I prefer to be at the helm of it, rather than feeling like I'm drifting in a lifeboat without any life support.

If I knew then what I know now, I would tell newly bereaved parents that the first year after loss is not the time to make drastic life changes. Hasty decisions or no decision at all are both a reaction to rapidly changing circumstances that are a given after child loss. When in doubt about what to do, they should wait things out and *only* make the changes they feel ready to make after a carefully considered plan. Even if that plan seems a little crazy, sometimes it's better to have that than no plan at all. Also, they should remember they can always change their mind.

I would warn them that after losing a child, it is common for many bereaved parents to suddenly quit or change jobs, have their relationship fall apart, face financial difficulties, lose interest in many things, see friends and even some family members fall by the wayside right after losing their child. This is all part of the trauma and grief.

They can also expect to experience family conflict and problems with surviving children. Despite how resilient people say kids are, dysfunctional kids grow into dysfunctional adults without some type of early intervention. Grieving parents need to remember they have living children for whom they are still responsible. Surviving siblings may be quick to think they should have been the child who died given all the outpouring of grief bereaved parents have for their lost sibling. Parents must remain on guard at all times for signs of trouble, unusual behavior, chronic illness or anything else out of the norm in surviving children and get them the help they need as quickly as possible. They should not let their surviving child tell them what they need. They won't know.

In our experience, my spouse and I tried to arrange counseling for our son through his doctor, school counselor and on our own for the many difficulties he was struggling with (anger, apathy, chronic health issues). All of our attempts failed miserably for several reasons. Not least that at age thirteen he already felt the stigma of his sister's suicide and was confused about whether or not he wanted to talk to anyone. He lived a double life. One, at home in the midst of our family grief and whirlwind of changes that left everyone feeling out of control. And everywhere else in complete secrecy about his sister's suicide (only two of his friends knew and both had attended the memorial with their parents). Our son didn't want to be seen as different from his peers. He was struggling to manage his emotions. To this day, he has never talked to us about his grief, though he did grow up to be stable and secure and a person I am incredibly proud to call my son.

Looking back, I regret not trying to find the right therapist trained in treating survivors of child and sibling suicide that would have included our son in part of the family's grief. With the right balance to include him, I feel certain this approach could have done much to eliminate the isolation he felt in his pain. Instead, we opted years later and at various times for relationship counseling. I would suggest to the newly bereaved that if therapy feels right for them, finding a therapist and therapy approach to help with family and relationship issues separately for right where they are in their individual grief, is essential. Issues that feel important or critical to address can and likely will change.

For anyone grieving the loss of a child, they will soon discover there is nothing anyone can say or do to soften the blows or protect them from the wretchedness of what they will face in their suffering. To lose all hope, motivation and trust in a brighter future is to be expected. Having to let go of the one they dreamed about isn't easy. In fact, it feels devastating to have everything snatched away in one moment in time. And, in the most shocking way they could ever have imagined.

I would tell newly bereaved parents that though the journey is long and filled with twists and turns, they can take comfort knowing that when the confusion clears, as it will, they can trust that they will find the courage to face every difficulty and steer themselves through all of the heartache. All of the growth. All of the healing.

Finally, I would suggest to the newly bereaved that they take their journey slow. To give themselves time to think about how they want to and can reshape their life at every stage of their grief. Most importantly, to remember to love themselves through it all.

Trauma and Post-Traumatic Stress Disorder

Dearest, darling girl. I have been avoiding writing about this topic. You see, I still struggle from the traumatizing effects of your choosing to leave this world. In no way would I ever make you wrong for choosing to leave, and it would be presumptuous of me to assume I know the reason why. Without you telling me, it's been an inner battle to try and figure out. A battle that no doubt is responsible for keeping me in a state I know is not good for my health. I hope that one day, sooner rather than later, I can give up my search for answers that all seems in vain anyway.

I have found over the years that most people don't understand trauma or relate it to loss. Though I did some early research and knew in my gut that bereaved parents should be included on the list of those who could suffer from Post-Traumatic Stress Disorder (PTSD), trauma and PTSD are not even discussed in relation to child loss. Yet, everyone knows that losing a child is traumatic. So, why people can't understand that bereaved parents can be afflicted with Post-Traumatic Stress Disorder too, is a mystery to me. It has been a long and difficult struggle living with PTSD, having not fully understood its impact on my life right from the start of my grief.

My diagnosis nearly ten years after your death brought me huge relief, but also the need to learn how to manage my symptoms to help improve my life all around. I also discovered it's not uncommon for sufferers of PTSD to be diagnosed years after the traumatic event occurred that was responsible for the disorder to manifest in their life.

Trauma compromises one's ability to feel alive. It keeps survivors in a constant state of hypervigilance to anything they perceive as a threat and unable to spontaneously engage in their daily life. While some trauma survivors may be able to adequately, if not expertly manage one or two parts of their life that give them the illusion of control (I found this to be true), largely they see themselves as damaged individuals and beyond redemption for their past mistakes. (I also found this to be true.)

I still remember instantly losing all feeling for even the smallest of things that had brought me so much pleasure before losing you, sweet daughter. The sound of birds singing. Seeing the first blooms of flowers in the garden I had loved so much. Feeling the warmth of the sun on my face or gazing at a clear blue sky. I no longer enjoyed family outings, nor could I feel the love of those around me.

Nothing except pain held meaning for me. I was frightened of everyone and everything. I wanted to stay in bed and never have to feel responsible for anything again. I sank into a deep depression amidst my ongoing struggle to rationalize many of the choices I was making for my life. They didn't make sense to me or those around me. I constantly beat myself up mentally and emotionally for not being the person I thought I should be or what I thought others wanted me to be, which only made me feel even more of a failure.

I was shocked to find myself in the situation our family was in. The more I struggled to find my place somewhere, anywhere, the more I lost all hope that things could ever be right in our lives again. I isolated myself from the outside world, convinced our family only had each other. It was like this for years.

The same as what happens to many families trying to survive a child's death, we were hit with secondary losses right from the beginning of our bereavement. Largely, these were financial, which is not uncommon when people can no longer work. In my earlier grief, the stress and worry I felt related to the mounting problems related to this and other issues compounded the PTSD symptoms I was struggling with that I didn't know I had. I was confused and frightened all of the time, not knowing what was happening to me or could happen at any given moment.

Understanding now that people living with PTSD experience confusion, fear, anxiety and paranoia and do not think rationally, I know that my overreactions to the enormous pressure I felt to fix all of our family's problems, and the terror I felt just thinking about having to go out into the world again to get a job were the direct result of PTSD. It wasn't because I was crazy like I thought (I'd read that many bereaved parents think they are going crazy in early grief but don't know why).

Corresponding online daily with other bereaved moms and survivors of suicide, though they weren't expressing this same foreboding and terror I was, it was clear we were all stumbling around in the dark trying to cope with our losses, supporting each other the best we could. While I didn't share with anyone my then very limited research into trauma and suspicions that grievers could have PTSD, especially after the loss of a child, I did share with them my ongoing struggle with various symptoms. These included recurring nightmares, continual flashbacks and insomnia, which they were experiencing too. In those early years, without any of us having any real understanding of trauma or PTSD, we were oblivious to the serious health risks that just a few symptoms can pose (there are many) and the devastation PTSD causes to every area of the trauma survivor's life.

My search for information years later and after my diagnosis helped me further understand that the behaviors of traumatized individuals are not the result of their lack of willpower, bad character or moral failings. They are caused by physiological changes in the brain, which was a huge relief to know. I instantly forgave myself all those earlier decisions I thought I should have made differently and recognized my gut reactions to problems were largely out of my control. It wasn't me deciding anything. Rather, it was my changed brain that was sending me warning signals of danger and prompting me to act to protect me or my loved ones from anything I perceived as a threat. Which was just about everything. Sometimes even the people closest to me.

My darling girl, thinking about some of the other devastating PTSD symptoms I experienced from the trauma of losing you, I try not to let myself go back too often to the years I spent haunted by images of what I imagined your final moments to be. What your actual death must have been like. I still get upset thinking about our final viewing of you at the funeral home. About your autopsy and what I was feeling at the exact moment you were being cremated. Of our last days and hours spent together before you died.

Those who acquire PTSD can expect to experience long-term, sudden triggers that take them back to the trauma they experienced right before and after their child's death. They can be haunted by memories, smells, photos, dates and tangible items, such as their child's clothing and other items to which they retain significant emotional attachment.

Though my reaction to these sorts of things are less intense today, there still are those things I can't bear to look at: your last letter to me, your baby pictures, your wallet and ID. These and sometimes even just the photos on the wall can instantly take me back to thoughts and feelings I'd rather not revisit. Usually, this is to the day you died and how things played out right before and after we discovered you were gone. It's like the trauma inside me has a life and purpose all its own to keep me locked in pain I can't escape from those few hours alone.

I won't rehash here the mistakes I made or regrets I have just from the day you died. They are explained elsewhere in these pages. I will say though, understanding now that my avoidance of many things and the heightened sensitivity I always feel are directly related to the trauma I experienced from your death, and the PTSD I now live with, has eased the pressure I once felt to quickly change myself from who I really am. Recognizing PTSD is a real health issue that must be managed, I've accepted that the healing I desire may not be entirely possible.

Anyone living with PTSD would no doubt agree that because the brain has been physiologically changed and the triggers of trauma are so unpredictable, it's questionable whether everyone can completely overcome PTSD. While some people do heal from PTSD, I've concluded that if I am to realize the best life possible, it may come down to whether I can recover from the trauma I still feel from losing you, and how well I manage the symptoms of Post-Traumatic Stress Disorder that continue to impact my life.

I'm not ashamed to admit my mental health struggles. I think it is likely more bereaved parents are impacted in this way, than not. To speak more openly about mental health in grief helps everyone affected feel more accepted and far less different than what they may consider others, just like them, are going through.

If I knew then what I know now, I would tell newly bereaved parents how critical it is to be aware of trauma and PTSD in grief and the potential risks of its effects. Because PTSD remains largely undiagnosed in grief, grievers must remain alert to health issues they believe may be the result of trauma or PTSD and immediately seek medical attention. Having a diagnosis can help them understand what they are experiencing and how to better manage their health.

In my view, there are two major reasons for the general lack of awareness about trauma and PTSD in grief. The first is a general lack of knowledge and information sharing about trauma and PTSD within the medical and grief support community. The second is the avoidance of grievers to reach out for help in their grief, where they may have the opportunity to share with professionals what they are experiencing and link it to trauma and PTSD. There are several reasons for this:

1. Even if a griever may suspect they are suffering from mental health issues that are grief-related, they may be afraid to ask for help.
2. They may not trust their doctor or a therapist enough to open up to them.
3. They may not have the energy to try and find the support they need.
4. Support may not be available where they live.
5. They may be confused about the kind of help they need.
6. They may lack the financial resources to see a therapist.
7. They may want to avoid the stigma related to mental health issues. It takes courage to ask for help.
8. They may not want to admit, even to themselves, that they are struggling with their mental health.

All of the bereaved parents I communicated with in early grief experienced many, if not all of the symptoms of PTSD. While for many, these likely would have dissipated over time, others may have acquired PTSD.

It is important bereaved parents understand that even though they may have experienced trauma, not everyone acquires PTSD. There are resources online to help individuals determine whether the symptoms they are experiencing are PTSD related. I strongly suggest they see their doctor and obtain a medical diagnosis to be certain. Their doctor should be able to recommend the proper resources to further assist them with support.

It takes insight, courage and perseverance to want to get and stay healthy after child loss. It is not a path that everyone chooses. Some bereaved parents do remain locked in their trauma and pain. My diagnosis of PTSD put in motion the events that ultimately led me to overhaul my life. While I initially resisted all that I would have to do to even start overhauling my life, I realized I am the only one responsible for how I want to live: with or without PTSD. Because I do want to get healthy, this means I've had to learn as much as I can about trauma and PTSD and make a concerted effort to manage my symptoms if I am to get the most out of my life. For example, often it is a matter of disciplining myself not to give in to my depression, anxiety, fear worry, illness and apathy where they rule my day. Having said this, I respect that my brain is now different. I don't push myself beyond my limits. I don't make myself feel wrong about anything I need or want or am currently experiencing.

While it feels cumbersome to have to manage our health in crisis, simply understanding early on that trauma is a very real part of child loss can encourage grievers coping with severe symptoms to confirm whether this may be PTSD, or they are the more common effects that every parent will experience after losing their child. PTSD symptoms are long-lasting. The individual will experience a combination of or all of these symptoms (there are others too):

1. Repeated disturbing memories or dreams.
2. Feeling like they are reliving the traumatic event over and over.
3. Strong physical reactions to reminders of the traumatic event.
4. Avoidance.
5. Memory loss.
6. A negative self-image.
7. Self-blame.
8. Feeling intense negative emotions such as fear, anger, guilt and shame.
9. A loss of interest in activities.
10. Isolation.
11. Taking risks.
12. Hypervigilance.
13. Insomnia or trouble sleeping.

Apart from getting the help they need early on, parents who are dealing with these types of symptoms or others and know for certain they are trauma or PTSD related, can stop making themselves feel wrong for having certain feelings or acting in ways that are uncharacteristic and even beyond their control.

There are various therapies professionals use to help people manage PTSD symptoms from a variety of traumatic events, including therapy with a focus on compassion. However, I've found with the research I've done, I've had to modify any of the therapy approaches to fit my grief experience. More research is needed to better inform those professionals dedicated to helping people recover from trauma about the specific type of treatment that bereaved parents need to recover from the trauma of losing their child.

In general, therapies to treat trauma include meditation, mindfulness, art, dance, yoga and music, self-soothing (the individual participates in activities they enjoy that feel soothing), cuddling with a live pet or stuffed animal, journaling. Additionally, therapists may use a number of other therapies in counseling. Some people take medication for a time. Personally, I've attended massage therapy to loosen my rigid body, have tried some energy healing treatments and regularly engage in self-soothing measures: I enjoy container gardening and live by the ocean and mountains which brings me peace.

It is my hope that bereaved parents suffering from trauma or living with PTSD will find the support they need a lot sooner than I did in my grief. While I am extremely grateful to have eventually found a doctor who recognized my PTSD symptoms, and was instrumental in helping me get the support that I needed to finally let go of who I could no longer be, it was an uphill battle that lasted for years before I eventually got this help. Right out of the gate of my bereavement there was no information to warn me of the possible effects of trauma in grief related to child loss. This needs to change.

Had I known early on in my grief about trauma and PTSD, I am certain our family could have been spared at least some of the suffering we endured for years. There was plenty of blame, misunderstandings and mistrust to go around that ultimately led to the emotional and sometimes physical isolation we experienced.

Grief is lonely enough without it being made more isolating and dangerous by health issues we don't understand. I would encourage the newly bereaved to see their doctor if they suspect they may have PTSD or are suffering other unmanageable effects from their trauma. It is essential to know the difference between the more common trauma effects in grief that do go away and the symptoms of PTSD that don't.

For anyone who does have PTSD, it is imperative they talk to their loved ones on a regular basis about what it's like for them to live with this disorder and what they need to feel supported. For family members, having to learn how to support a loved one living with PTSD is no different than having to learn how to support the needs of a loved one experiencing any other type of health issue. However, I do feel that living with PTSD in grief, and as a less talked about health issue, requires that loved ones are properly educated about the disorder to help them better support those needing their care. I've found it a lonely affliction to live with.

Grief requires that individuals who stay together must work together. Everyone must respect the journey of their loved ones in grief. When it comes to PTSD, loved ones must be willing to help the one afflicted manage the disorder by understanding the nature of the symptoms, and treating the sufferer with compassion and kindness at all times. Whether this is a partner, children or even extended family members, it's true that when one person has PTSD, everyone suffers. But, it's also true that when someone with PTSD begins to recover, everyone benefits from their healing.

For information about online resources related to trauma and PTSD, please see "Trauma" under Resources at the back of this book.

Gratitude

Gratitude is the quality one has of being able to feel deeply appreciative, thankful or grateful for all that they have or are about to receive. Whether this is related to an act of kindness, new situation, relationship, baby, house, job and anything else one appreciates as a blessing or abundance, there is an overwhelming feeling of contentment and joy that accompanies the feeling of gratitude.

Like many other consciousness-raising practices, there are different approaches to how one thinks about and expresses gratitude. For me, sweet daughter, the gratitude I felt for years when you were alive no longer holds the same meaning for me since you've been gone. To feel gratitude for anything requires something I no longer have; which is an appreciation for everything in my life despite all that has befallen me.

It was terribly difficult in those first years after you died for me to even want to feel grateful for anything, let alone find one thing in my heart that could make me feel this way again. While for the most part, I could intellectually accept our family's changed circumstances, hardly would I say I felt an appreciation for them. Not even when I could admit, if only to myself, the importance of my lessons that I'm certain could only have resulted from your leaving. I still feel challenged to some extent to appreciate all that I have, though I no longer try to force myself to feel a deep appreciation for my life or portray myself as someone with that former sunny attitude I once had.

Because sincere gratitude comes from a deep place inside of us and is something that can't be faked, I have taken time to ponder its true meaning for me in my bereavement. When and if I can regain a feeling of gratitude for my life; the way I felt being a mom to you and your brother (I do still feel this way about your brother), I'd like for it to come from an appreciation I can feel just from having had you in my life. When I can feel this, I am certain I will once again be able to have an appreciation for my life as it is today and all that's yet to come. Perhaps, too tall an order still, given how much I've struggled with your absence.

Earlier in these pages and in speaking about joy, I contemplated whether our ability to create lasting joy may come from simply *wanting* to feel gratitude for all of our experiences. As I believe that joy and gratitude go hand in hand (you can't have one without the other), I think a lot about whether those few moments I can cherish whenever the feeling of gratitude stirs within me, will one day turn into that longer lasting feeling I'd like to have that would help me feel enamoured by life once again. I can feel a pleasing, soothing sensation just thinking about it.

But then, I get bogged down by unanswered questions every time I look at your photo or a memory surfaces from when you were alive that challenges me to feel thankful for the happy times we had together and grateful you were in my life, no matter for how long. I can feel my innards twist with a pain that's still so hard to let go of.

I sometimes feel like a cat chasing my tail when I think about all the emotional damage that I'd like to no longer feel; all of it related to your death. But it's been impossible to make the pain go away. The only thing that feels remotely sane about losing you is the belief I hold onto that I did choose all these lessons and you were the one to teach me, both before and after you died. I should feel grateful. Yet, I can't. Pain I can't let go of keeps me from appreciating the enormous sacrifice we both made for the things I've learned that in retrospect, sometimes don't really seem that important.

While this particular way of looking at your death has helped me cope, I also think if I could just appreciate it for its truth that this would set me free. At least, freer than what I currently feel in every state of my being.

I really am trying to see things differently and to accept that your death happened for a reason. That it was in perfect timing with how our lives were meant to be. That I couldn't have done anything differently to save you. That it wasn't my role to save you. That not having the knowledge then that I do now was always part of the greater plan.

There are some things I think about that I feel would be considerably better for my healing to believe. Yet, I can't change every thought and belief I have overnight, if at all. Those that are within my grasp to understand differently, I can assure you, I am making a sincere effort to do so. At the top of my list: acquiring an appreciation for the life I've led and still have before me, despite it being likely I will never really understand what took you from me.

I believe that every bereaved parent faces the same challenge to fully accept their child's death, whatever the cause or manner. I remember having a conversation with a group of grieving parents not long after you died about whether we'd do it all again, just to have those few precious years back with each of you. There was a resounding yes from the collective, but I stayed silent. I honestly didn't know. I've thought about that conversation a lot ever since.

It's not that I didn't (and don't) love you enough to want to do it all again. It's just that knowing the ending keeps me from answering this question with a resounding yes! Perhaps I'm not far enough along in my healing to have acquired this same appreciation for the years we had together that other bereaved parents have when thinking about their lost child. Or, maybe it's because in choosing your own death and without leaving me an explanation, you left me with a suffering that feels intolerable because I'll never know the answer to my question about why you chose to die. Which has complicated my efforts to release you to the past and me to move beyond this painful part of my grief.

Certainly, I feel grateful for all that you have taught me, both in and beyond your presence in this physical world. But the gratitude I want to be able to express is from how lucky and blessed I feel just having had you in my life. I wanted it to have been longer.

If I knew then what I know now, I would tell newly bereaved parents that surviving their child's suicide is a journey fraught with problems that no one can relate to who hasn't gone through it. They are the result of a loss so great that nobody else wants to contemplate it, and from a manner of death that can't ever be understood by anyone. Least of all parents and the surviving family. Suicide on its own, never mind the suicide of a child or young adult, leaves many people struggling for years with questions that can never be answered. It's a messy type of grief.

I would suggest to any parent trying to survive the suicide of their child that there may be no other way to deal with the aftermath than by challenging themselves to think more deeply about their loss after sufficient time has passed. A deeper questioning of their child's death and their subsequent grief, while not necessarily the means to overcoming pain entirely, can ease some of the suffering that otherwise may not ever go away. Having an understanding of their child's death that makes sense to the bereaved parents can help them at least try to accept the death. Though honestly, with suicide, I'm not sure if this is even possible.

Many people live with unresolved pain for various reasons. Finding ways to overcome their suffering is what gives everyone their unique experience in grief. I have always believed that knowing the cause of any problem is half the solution. Pain is no different. Understanding how and why we hurt gives to us the means to see and do things differently.

Regarding gratitude, for any bereaved parent desiring to acquire an appreciation for all of their life that includes the acceptance of their child's death, I would encourage them to remember that just wanting to feel grateful for *anything* in their grief is a sign of hope. Being able to see a tiny beacon of light at the end of a dark tunnel hints to them there can be a better future one day. It can be critical in their healing for newly bereaved parents to hold onto any spark of light they can imagine when they are feeling overwhelmed by the surrounding darkness.

Thinking about my earliest grief, I am so grateful now that I found the strength then to get out of bed, move my body a little (I did gentle yoga at home), email my bereaved friends I'd met online for daily support, and find the will and energy to love and care for my son through all of my suffering. In large part, it was because of him that I was able to dig deep to search for and find greater meaning in my life after losing his sister. As bad as the experience was, and it is one I would never want to repeat, things could have been much worse.

While being able to feel gratitude for any small thing in grief can be tough for any bereaved parent, those new to grief may find as I did that the loss and grief experience is really more about their story than what they could ever hope to rewrite for their lost child. It took me years to understand this. For anyone focusing on their loss alone, they will never get the ending they want. It is painful trying. Their longing will keep them tied to their suffering.

Despite knowing this, it's also true that it will be really hard to let go of everything they had dreamed for their child. For their family. For themselves. Being able to feel gratitude for their life in their bereavement, I believe comes more from being able to see their loss and grief in a way that doesn't feel as punishing than perhaps what they are used to, which requires being gentle with themselves every step of their journey.

Perseverance

Well darling girl, I have been nothing if not persistent in my efforts to get through this thing called grief. I know how proud of me you'd be if you were here. Not that I ever gave up on anything, but this is one doozy of a challenge keeping me on my toes. Pushing me to always go beyond my comfort zone.

There are days I feel really proud of myself for persevering against all odds in my effort to always make things better. To get healthy. To enjoy my relationships without there always having to be strain. To always be learning so that I can better understand my experience here on earth before I die. Without perseverance, I'm not sure where or who I'd be right now. The grief from child loss really messes you up.

Of course, as soon as I say this, I feel an immediate urge to quickly find solutions to all of my problems so that life can get back to being as normal as it could be. But then I remember - it's not normal to lose a child. And as fast as I think I should be able to find the answers to all of my burning questions that would resolve my lingering pain, I feel myself as vulnerable now as I did before sliding down that rabbit hole. To a darkness that is very easy to get stuck in.

I know because it happens to people who haven't dealt with their inner turmoil from whatever pain they are experiencing. They end up alone and lost, without anything or anyone that once mattered to them. I realized very early in my bereavement how quickly the same fate could befall any one of us struggling with pain that is so much bigger than ourselves.

Not from day one right after your death, did I ever want to end up feeling lost and alone. Not when all the commotion was over and there were no more people coming and going from the house. Not when the dust had settled, and I was left utterly alone to try and understand what truly lay ahead. Not through all of my grief to this point.

There is a saying ... *but for the grace of God go I.* So, whether it was from my childhood years raised in a Christian environment or later ones, when I became heavily involved in my spiritual practice but where faith is key in both, in as sane a way possible, I thought a lot in those early days about what I didn't want for my life. At the heart of this was the terror I felt not knowing how I was going to survive the rest of my life without you and what it was going to take to keep me on this planet.

I saw no other way through the pain than to find the strength and a will I'd never had to think about before not to *ever* allow myself to succumb to my misery and all that I imagined this would entail. I figured if suffering was all there was in grief, I'd end up dead for sure.

Instinctively wanting to avoid a darker path that seemed more terrifying than the one I was already on, I strove daily, to try and feel a little spark of good or hope or something; anything that would push me to keep breathing. Moving. Surviving. It was like this for years. In fact, this survival instinct still pushes me to some degree today.

I wish I could tell those new to this path that recovering from the loss of their child was guaranteed if they could only tap into that one magic formula that has gotten every bereaved parent through the ordeal. But finding what this is leaves every one of us searching. I read as many books as I could on child loss right after you died, sweet child. I wanted to know what I was in for from those that had gone before me. But there weren't that many books and even fewer answers. All but one I read had been written by grieving dads. None had lost their child to suicide.

Disregarding that the manner of death for their children was different (mostly natural), I read through each page and felt the pain they still carried with every written word. And, while most of what I read didn't give me much hope for a better future, I did take comfort knowing I was not alone in my grief. Still, I wondered about the moms. Why weren't they writing about their grief? What were they going through? I thought it had to be different than grieving fathers.

Over the years I've struggled to remain optimistic that every bereaved parent can come out of their child loss experience stronger, wiser and feeling more positive. But as the years go by, I just don't see it. Do we gain wisdom? Yes. But do any of us feel stronger and more positive? I haven't found this in my experience or the experience of any bereaved parent I've ever met. No one I've ever met has been beaming with a joy and love of life itself. Every face betrays what any of us might otherwise be telling other people and maybe even ourselves. No parent I've ever met has ever proclaimed to be healed. They all have only said that things are now different, even many years after losing their child.

Thinking now about what could possibly help someone survive losing their child in a less horrible way than most of us do, perhaps finding some purpose in the despair is the best motivator. Having purpose pushes us to slog through what can seem like endless inner turmoil, even on the best days.

Though I started out wanting to do and be all that I could become as a way to pay tribute to you my darling girl, I have since discovered that if I am to heal, at some point I have to want a life for me. It's doubtful that wherever you now are, you are consumed by anything that I continue to struggle with.

If I knew then what I know now, I would tell newly bereaved parents to take each day as it comes and leave the worry behind them as much as they can, especially in their early grief. While this is easier said than done, if they can avoid putting pressure on themselves to take on more than what they can handle, it will go a long way to helping them obtain the balance and perspective they will need in grief.

Every bereaved parent must persevere throughout all of their grief in many ways. Initially, just having the discipline to get up and face each new day with the courage it takes to keep going - sometimes minute by minute; breath by breath, is the only thing that will see them through their darkest hours. As time progresses, they will feel challenged by many things. Persisting in a simple course of action to meet each new challenge can provide some structure and bring them a feeling of organization amidst the chaos.

This can be especially helpful to remember when having to deal with incredibly difficult things in the first few days and weeks after their child's death, such as: notifying family and friends, their child's school, employer and various institutions of the death, arranging the funeral or memorial, closing their child's bank and other business or personal accounts, putting away their child's clothing and items, dismantling their bedroom or removing items from the home they lived in, deciding what to keep or give away.

While these tasks are largely entrusted to parents of a dependent child or young adult who has died and where they retain legal responsibility, it is important to remember that a child of any age could fall into this category. And every parent, no matter their legal responsibility, feels the same about their child's death at any age.

I would tell newly bereaved parents to expect settling into their grief to take weeks, if not months. Rest is important. Focusing on one goal at a time can reduce the overwhelm they may feel having to deal with obligations that still must be met, no matter what state they are in. Dividing the day into three parts (morning, afternoon, evening) can reduce the agony of surviving what feels like endless hours of suffering from a very real slowdown of time that does occur during this initial period of grief.

It is important that grieving parents remember to feel proud of themselves for anything they can accomplish at any stage in their grief. At first, this may be brushing their hair and teeth, caring for surviving children, feeding a pet, walking a dog, taking a bath or shower, getting dressed. Bigger accomplishments, such as a return to work and introducing other routines into their life, that while they take longer to resume and even are expected, should still be recognized as major accomplishments when they do occur. I would encourage the newly bereaved not to rush their early grief process. They can trust that in time they will be able to strive for more.

Finally, I would tell anyone on this difficult path that given the enormity of the journey ahead that for everyone is filled with ups and downs and twists and turns, not to worry or fear they'll never be able to do what must be done. With perseverance, they will always find a way to meet each new challenge head on. To keep themselves on their path to healing. To find meaning in their experience.

Isolation

There is a danger in experiencing pain so great that we become isolated from others, but that is exactly what happens when we lose a child. We may even become dissociated from parts of ourselves, for example to our past. To who we used to be. To our memories. Who else, but those who have experienced a child's death could possibly understand the isolation we feel when we are now so different from everyone else?

Before you died, sweet daughter, I remember watching the odd movie that centered on a child's death and the agony the parents went through. Even talking years ago to two moms who unexpectedly told me of their losses (both had lost a young child), just like anyone who has not experienced this, I couldn't relate to their pain. I watched the movies and listened to these bereaved moms with what I thought was just the right amount of sympathy, but in truth, I was completely detached emotionally because I couldn't imagine what they must be going through. I had no concept of either mom's grief. No one had died in our family. I didn't know a thing about grief.

The barrier that exists between those who have experienced child loss and everyone else has silenced our culture on the topic of child death. This makes the grief complicated for grieving parents and their families. In addition, the lack of understanding and stigma of suicide further complicates the parent bereavement experience. It naturally creates this feeling of isolation within us because we feel and are so different from others. It's natural to think that something went wrong with the family. With our child. Maybe even with our parenting. There are a host of thoughts that will consume us after losing our child to suicide that will keep us feeling isolated in one way or another.

In terms of how difficult it is to understand grief from child loss and try to support bereaved parents, imagine going to a country where you don't know the language. In many cultures, just getting the gestures, tones and pronunciation of certain words wrong can be an insult to the local hosts. They are not likely to demonstrate a welcoming attitude or offer their best service. And, if you were to find yourself in a country where communication is not possible, until you learn some of the basic local words and gestures, you would likely have difficulty trying to communicate your needs and maybe even get help, at least not without a translator.

For many travelers, one of the first questions they may ask a local resident is whether they speak the traveler's language. While many people may know a handful of words in one of the universal languages, the best practice for anyone preparing to travel to a foreign country is to learn the customs and a few key phrases before arriving at their destination, which can help them ingratiate themselves with the local people. They will for sure be treated in kind with respect and kindness, which can make the travel experience more rewarding and memorable. Having traveled, lived and worked abroad I know this to be true.

While admittedly, it takes effort to learn the customs and a few words of a foreign country and it may be easier to find a translator when necessary; alternatively, people may choose to travel only to places where they know their own language is spoken. While this is okay, it is far less adventurous and diminishes the opportunity for one's personal awareness and growth.

The point is that in many cultures, even when you can't communicate in the local language, most people are thrilled when visitors make an attempt to communicate with them and know a little bit about their culture. Happy people make happy hosts. I've often found that with a just a little effort to speak with people and ask them about their culture, many local residents are appreciative and quick to offer their best service. They often go above and beyond to help out.

In many ways, grief from child loss is the same. Living as a local in this alternate world, I've found trying to communicate my needs to people who don't speak my language and are too afraid to learn about child loss has been one of the most difficult things in my grief. I've felt like an outsider in mainstream society for years. Those who do want to help don't know how. I'm not even sure anymore what I would need or want from them because I've been shut down for so long. I've gotten used to managing alone when it comes to coping with the deeply personal issues that I still struggle with and most people can't relate to.

In all ways, the grief experience feels vastly different from the majority of challenging life events we all can expect to face at some point in our lives. While my frustration is not meant to disparage others and I know I'll never be alone in my grief, the reality is that being thrust into a world that few people understand after losing you, sweet girl, is lonely and isolating. I haven't yet found a way to make it seem less so.

I know that with every other difficult life event I've encountered and survived, the ability we have to connect with others and share what we are going through influences how we are feeling. When we feel better about ourselves, we can recover from the experience. The isolation of grief after child loss prevents us from connecting to others and fulfilling some of our most basic needs as a human being. That is to feel safe and that we belong, which helps us develop self-esteem and the desire to reach our full potential.

When we struggle through life alone feeling undervalued, misunderstood, unsupported and unloved, so much of what we feel we can do and who we can be disappears. It's as though we have no potential at all. In whatever way we experience isolation; emotionally, physically or both, it negatively impacts what we believe about ourselves and squashes our desire to pursue too much of anything, including getting healthy. It's a risky place to be. Pain can become a dangerous companion if it's our only one.

While this may sound dire, after child loss anything in grief can negatively impact the bereaved parent. The risk to all areas of our well-being should not be underestimated. I was dangerously close to cutting myself off from everyone and everything after you died, my darling girl. Circumstances forced me back into the world a few months later. While I was angry at the time, I see now that this may have inadvertently led me away from the overwhelming temptation that I felt to lock myself inside my house and head.

If I knew then what I know now, I would tell newly bereaved parents to expect to feel misunderstood and not fully supported in their grief. While I wish things were different, years after the start of my own bereavement I've found that they are not. This is nobody's fault. Part of the problem may be that not understanding what we are going through as bereaved parents, does nothing to help remove the barriers between us and the rest of the world. Asking for help can educate professionals about what we need. Yet, the cultural silence around child loss and related grief that can be attributed in part to our abhorrence to think and talk about the death of other people's children, prevents many bereaved parents from reaching out for help. Not being able to freely talk about child death and the grief of bereaved parents translates into insufficient education, information about and support systems for the majority of bereaved parents and their families. And I believe this to be particularly true where the manner of death is suicide.

Being thrust into my first experience of grief from the suicide of my child was shocking. My feelings were a jumbled mess, but prominent among them was the certainty that I had failed as a parent. This immediately set me apart in my mind from parents who still had their kids, which was the majority. The regrets and what ifs consumed me for years (they sometimes still can). To overcome the stigma and embarrassment I felt about my perceived failings as a parent, I simply decided one day to not let them be a stigma. In truth, I never likely was judged by anyone. I would encourage others who may be struggling with this belief to let it go too. There are bigger things to worry about.

In fact, when I think about how many children, young adults and older adults are dying by suicide every day, any stigma we may be feeling about ourselves as failures in any way is ours alone to feel. The rate at which we are hearing about these deaths is staggering. Suicide is considered a national crisis in many countries. While we are no longer avoiding talking about suicide, we have failed in every respect to understand the reasons why people take their life and ending this ongoing crisis. However tragic and heartbreaking the experience, none of us will ever have to feel alone from having lost our child to suicide. The isolation we feel is more in the grief experience itself.

I've thought a lot over the years about what difference even a little acknowledgement and respect for bereaved parents' grief could have made (or would still make) to my healing. Whenever I've had the opportunity to share a few details about my life with people who have legitimately been interested in chatting, including sharing with them that I had a daughter but she died, I've always come away from the exchange feeling more hopeful and encouraged because I don't feel so alone. They are people just like me with issues of their own. It feels comforting and far less isolating when we can remember that we're all in life together, no matter that our struggles may be different.

Death is not discriminating. The loss of a child can happen to anyone, any time. This may be helpful for people to remember instead of fear to remove at least part of the cultural stigma surrounding suicide. Also, it is important that as bereaved parents, we remember that no parent is perfect. We all make mistakes. For those of us with surviving children who are doing well, it's worth considering that it can't have been our parenting alone, if at all, that was the reason for our lost child's death.

Finally, I would remind everyone just how incredible it would feel to us all if the sensitivity, empathy and compassion people can feel for their own loved ones' suffering could be just as easily transferred to the suffering felt by so many others. No one can ever really know the positive impact that just a small amount of compassion demonstrated can have on anyone around them.

Support

Discussing support ties in beautifully with all I've said about isolation. I'm not really sure you can have one and not the other. In grief, you either feel totally supported and not isolated, or totally isolated and not supported. Perhaps there is a middle ground, but if I were to be totally honest, in my experience I'd say no.

I don't know what it's like to feel totally loved and supported since you died, sweet daughter. Maybe no bereaved parent does. I still get frustrated and overreact sometimes to the words and actions of others. Which isn't really fair to anyone, given that people, including loved ones, don't know how to support me. Life for them is a far cry from what I am always struggling with.

Despite my constant search to find ways to end all of my pain, which now includes me having to strictly manage my health, environment and relationships, with regard to the latter, I've come to accept that I cannot change the attitude or behavior of others towards me or themselves in their own pain. I can't change anyone, regardless of their life experience, who doesn't have the innate ability to feel kindness and compassion for anyone going through the most horrific experience of their life. For me, this was losing you, my beautiful girl. For others just like me, it's been from losing their own precious child.

We all need love, compassion and support in our suffering, but I've found that people can only relate to those with whom they share similar experiences. Because of this lack of support, I sometimes feel angry about the insensitivity of others and how I sense they are (or aren't) treating me. Often in the mainstream world, I felt there were many demands placed on me with the expectation I was someone with much more capability than I really felt I had. While I understand why most people wouldn't see me as someone who has been so damaged because of how I carry and present myself, I know for a fact that bereaved and non-bereaved individuals are worlds apart in how we view and cope with life. This is especially true for parents who have lost a child.

In general, those with no clue about grief have, well, no clue. Those who have experienced loss of some type are empathetic and compassionate, but still miss in a large way the true suffering that comes with losing a child. I do, however, feel a connection to anyone who has experienced grief in some way because I know that what we suffer after loss is partly the same for everyone. It's just that losing a child is a whole different ball game.

You, my darling girl, were part of my DNA. A part of all the same substances keeping me alive today, although sometimes in such unbearable pain. All of which I manage to hide from everyone.

As your mom, I've believed for years that letting go of you was necessary if I am to fully heal. But, because I still can feel this same invisible cord attaching me to you that all moms have to their children, I'm not so sure anymore. Maybe this is why letting you go has been so difficult. Perhaps, and different to what I previously thought, surrendering my hold on you won't be so easy, if at all possible, because this cord cannot be severed. It's something to think about for sure.

Closing my eyes, I can see a beautiful silver line that is attaching us. If one could see this for themselves, it might look like either a light or dark sky full of silver cords so thin they appear as nothing more than wisps of brilliance throughout an otherwise vast space. Perhaps it is these wisps I see that represent the infinite love every bereaved parent still has for every child who has been lost but must still exist in some way. In the same way you must all continue to exist beyond being just a memory for some. I am going to hang on to this vision because it feels comforting in my otherwise, often lonely existence.

Trying to imagine the heartache and loneliness of grief for bereaved parents is difficult for those who have not experienced it. No wonder we feel so unsupported. Maybe not even thought about past the initial onslaught of visitors that arrive at our door at the very beginning of our grief.

Recently, I watched a motivational speaker online. Discussing trauma in general, she recalled the honor she felt sitting with people affected by mass shootings, genocide or loss of their child. That caught my attention. Did I hear right that someone was actually including the unimaginable trauma experienced from the loss of a child as being on the same scale as people who have witnessed genocide? It's debatable in my view whether putting these two in the same trauma category further serves to alienate the child loss experience, because most of us could never imagine witnessing let alone surviving genocide, or gives bereaved parents the proper acknowledgement they deserve from the very real suffering that all bereaved parents mostly endure alone and in silence.

Whatever the case, child loss talked about in this context helps me understand even more why the support I've desperately wanted is likely always going to be arm's length at best for the simple reason that people just don't get it. They can't get it. As bereaved parents we shouldn't expect them to get it (most bereaved parents probably don't). Child loss is something so devastating it can only be imagined by people. The majority don't even want to do that.

I know. I used to be just like them. It's too close for comfort to imagine anything so horrific that any parent knows deep down they could experience, too.

If I knew then what I know now, I would tell newly bereaved parents that any hope they may have to feel understood and supported by others may be in vain. Comprehending child loss in general, but especially from suicide is a long and difficult process for everyone affected by that loss. For the bereaved parent, it's a double whammy not only trying to cope with their child's death, but for most, trying to understand the reason their child chose to die. It's a journey filled with twists and turns. You never know what you may be up against because of the severe emotional damage that can leave every suicide survivor at risk of complications in their grief that cannot be easily or quickly fixed.

I found support early in my grief by connecting with other bereaved parents online and attending a support group in person. I also read as much as I could on the subject. Those new to child loss may find comfort reading books written by bereaved parents or attending a support group in person like *The Compassionate Friends*. *The Compassionate Friends* has chapters around the world and is dedicated to helping bereaved parents from their earliest grief. Additionally, they may be able to find a suicide support group in their area that has a subgroup exclusive to parents who have lost a child to suicide. There are also online grief groups and communities. It is important to remember that support groups are there to help, but like anything else, it is essential that bereaved parents find a group or online community that feels right for them.

For newly bereaved parents that choose to go it alone, they may find it more difficult to settle into their grief. I've encountered many bereaved parents over the years who never got help. While this remains a personal choice, I found early on and maintain today that there is comfort and healing in connecting and sharing. Having said this, it's important to note that support may be hard to find, depending on where you live. In Canada, support groups dedicated to helping bereaved parents who have lost a child to suicide and younger sibling survivors of a suicide are rare, if they even exist. Grief support groups in general are spread very thinly across the nation.

My experience over the years has taught me that many people hold their grief close to their heart. They don't share their pain with others. There may be a number of reasons for this. Not least, they may not understand what they are feeling or how to express their pain. It can be generational too, where people of a certain age were taught not to dwell on their loss and pain.

In general, we don't live in a society in the west that is overly supportive of loss and grief and not at all when it comes to getting help for surviving the suicide of our children. My daughter died in 2005. Because I have been vocal throughout my grief mostly through my writing and some speaking engagements, I am very aware of the silence around grief from child loss. Today, the same as when I first became bereaved, I can confidently say there are not enough voices being raised or heard to bring about the changes we need to improve the support that all grieving parents need. The grief bereaved parents struggle with can last forever. It can be directly attributed to the many additional losses that grievers experience: health issues, relationships breaking down, job loss, financial hardship, problems with their surviving children.

The needs of bereaved parents constantly change and are reflected by whatever is happening in any area of their life. Upsetting triggers will never be far away. The sooner bereaved parents know what they are struggling with the more aware they'll be of the changes they need to make to survive the trauma and chaos. Even when they can't make these changes just yet.

Being attuned to what they are thinking and feeling at all times in their grief can go a long way to sorting out many of the problems that arise. As they begin to sift through the residue of what they've been left with after the death of their child, bereaved parents at every stage in their grief will be able to gain a clearer understanding of all that they and their family have been through, which will have been phenomenal. What they choose to do with the knowledge at hand will be pivotal in how they move forward.

I would tell newly bereaved parents and those still struggling with grief that from my experience, the number one rule in healing is to know thyself first. It is impossible for anyone wanting to help them to guess at what they are feeling and need. This includes loved ones, friends, colleagues, employers, therapists and other medical professionals.

Learning about grief related to child loss through books, local or online support groups (I made many friends online with whom I communicated daily), journaling their thoughts and feelings, praying, meditating, taking personal development courses, attending church, developing an interest in spirituality, can help them develop a fuller understanding of their experience. Whatever connects them to their truth will be critical to their healing.

Awareness brings us out of the darkness. As much as I wanted my healing to come through other people, this was not the case. From the beginning of my grief I wanted someone to wave a magic wand and make all my pain go away. They can't. Ultimately, we are our own best support, though it's important to know when to reach out for help and whom to ask.

I still believe that at the core of all healing is the will anyone has to want to get better. Though by now everyone reading this book knows it is so much more complicated than that, having the courage to tell their partner, other loved ones and anyone else in their close circle what they need and want is half the battle to getting the support they need. With faith, all bereaved parents can carry themselves through all of the rest.

For information about online resources related to support, please see "Support" under Resources at the back of this book.

Desire

Desire is that which we long for that brings us satisfaction or enjoyment. When it comes to feeling desire for anything, I have been left with an inner void since you died, sweet daughter. All that I ever wanted when you were alive was for you, and our family, to be happy and to realize every desire that each of us had. Boy, did that blow up in my face!

Since your death, I have been careful not to desire too much of anything, having learned the hard way how quickly it all can be taken away from us. As the years have passed, and while at times I've found myself somewhat excited by some opportunity that has enticed me to keep moving forward (though towards what I've never really felt certain), the important thing is I've kept moving.

There was a time I really did believe that I could heal from all my pain, and with this, would follow my burning desire to go after whatever I dreamed possible. But I have found that my dreaming and any feeling I could have to desire much of anything has been greatly impacted by my grief. Not gone entirely from my mind and heart, because if they were, I'm not sure I'd still be here. Perhaps desire is partly what keeps us motivated and living. Still, saying this, I'd never discourage anyone from believing that they can retain their ability to dream and feel desire in their grief.

Sometimes I think that if I were to have a tombstone, I'd want the epitaph to read *try, try again* because that is exactly what I feel I've had to do all these long years since your death. Whatever I'm striving to achieve seems to have eluded me. It seems like any gains I make continue to be overshadowed by the challenges I still face. This is probably not entirely true, but it is how I feel.

And then, I remind myself how lucky I am to have what's left of our family. Beaten down for sure, but still intact. For this, I should feel grateful that at least part of the desire I once had does remain, even though I struggle to believe there still can be so much more to life. Which surely, if I did believe, would fuel a host of desires I could feel that would give me that zest for life again. In truth, the only desire I've had since you died was that your death would not ever be a waste. I've always wanted something good to come from it. I'm certain most bereaved parents feel the same way.

Whatever I have learned from your passing, I have tried to make it count by sharing it with others. With my only real goal being this, I've never wanted to pursue anything that seems insincere or fleeting. The success I've felt in what I've done and believe I could still accomplish has always wavered. I've felt disadvantaged by my grief and often challenged to stay the course. Deep down, I struggle to imagine what could possibly make me want anything other than to have you back? Which I'm sure has put a damper on my ability to feel desire in general.

Sometimes I wonder if I'm the only bereaved parent that feels this way, but I don't think so. I think all bereaved parents desire that their life be different. That they could have their child back. Oh, to have just a minute with you again!

Perhaps it's time I looked at desire from an altogether different perspective. Maybe it should have nothing to do with achievement, but rather the desire I can summon just to be the best I can be at any given moment. Maybe this is sufficient expectation for every bereaved parent.

I admit this approach feels much less pressured than thinking about desire in the way that we are used to. Which is the longing for and striving to achieve many things and experiences we don't yet have.

In my grief, I used to place a lot more emphasis on my desire to attain the peace and contentment I thought would result from my healing. But, given I haven't been able to fully achieve any of these things yet, I wonder if I've been holding myself to too high a standard, and for so long, that this in itself has beaten me down. The longer I've been in grief the more complicated it has become.

In thinking about desire in general, I have to wonder that without it, what type of life can we expect to have? As human beings, it is part of our basic nature that we feel desire and strive to achieve our full potential. To not test the limits of our capabilities may well seem a testament to our laziness, disinterest or suffering. And who wants to live out their life defined by any of these three?

If I knew then what I know now, I can honestly say I wish I'd known immediately upon the death of my daughter that I could never again expect to be who I was. I think I spent a few years trying, at least in my head. I would caution the newly bereaved to expect that the desire they may feel for anything will diminish greatly, if not disappear altogether in their grief. At least for a time. All that they have known will have vanished. For those who have never experienced grief, they will be stumbling around in a foreign world without a map.

Every new bereaved parent must start their life over again, taking the time to discover who they are and what they want. It's a long road. To feel desire for things that will bring them satisfaction and enjoyment likely will be way down on their list of things they will hope to achieve as they struggle to survive each day.

Every experience in grief is unique to the individual who is grieving and will be based on their past and current experiences, environment and relationships. Yet, within the context of emotional suffering, emotions are generic to us all, though we may not experience or react to them the same way.

Every time I have spoken about our experiences in grief with other bereaved parents it is not surprising that we feel more the same about having lost our child than different. Nobody I've ever met or read about has felt or been the same as before their child's death. I've considered that the shock of our child's death can even trigger us to experience something similar to what partial temporary amnesia may be like, where you no longer know who you are and nothing makes sense, even though you recognize your surroundings.

For instance, I have a few memories before our D Day (the date of my daughter's death). But most are fuzzy and how I now remember them may not be the same as if my daughter were still alive. It feels as though I'm remembering someone else's life, rather than my own. I've considered this is from the trauma and my mind shielding me from anything that could make the pain I feel today, even worse.

Having no desire to linger in the past anyway, I would tell newly bereaved parents that when they can feel a desire for more, wanting anything for their future is likely healthier than only desiring what they can't have from the past. But like everything else in grief for all bereaved parents, we have to let things go when we are ready.

I've struggled with the idea that when I can review my past without any desire for my life to be different, it will represent a whole new relationship I want to have with my daughter; even if this can only be in mind and heart. But because I can't imagine yet what this would be, I cling to the past and all I knew and can remember that is still overwhelmingly painful to think about.

With regard to talking about desire in general, I would tell the newly bereaved to expect desires to come and go, depending on where they are in their grief. Initially, they may desire only to have some solitude and quiet, to sleep, to have help with the kids, pets or other responsibilities. To not feel so crushed from the death of their child.

As they progress through grief and remembering that desire in a general sense is longing for something that will bring them satisfaction or enjoyment, their desires will shift to the external. Maybe this will be to buy or try something new. Return to a former hobby, travel or socialize again. Bereaved parents shouldn't be hard on themselves for wanting to enjoy themselves. I've met many grieving parents who believed, at least in the early years, that they shouldn't feel pleasure.

In any event, what any bereaved parent may desire throughout their grief will be based on their ability to feel and want certain things. These will largely be dependent on the state of their health and relationships, home, family, work and social environments.

Suicide & Stigma

I t's strange that we don't talk about stigma itself, which refers to disgrace or the stain on one's reputation. There is even a medical definition that describes stigma as a mental or physical mark characteristic of a defect or disease.

When you think about the stigma of suicide that still exists, never mind that we are talking about suicide more socially even in a limited context: that is, almost every suicide is attributed to mental illness, how can those of us parents who have been directly impacted by the suicide of our child not help but feel we have some sort of defect or that there now is a stain upon our character? Right there alongside our child? Or anyone for that matter who has died by suicide?

Since my early grief, I've tried to bring awareness to the idea that suicide is about so much more than attributing it only to mental illness. In fact, when you look at the hundreds of thousands of suicides of intelligent and capable people, where nobody has suspected any cause for alarm, it makes me think that not everyone who has killed themselves have done so impulsively or because they've gone mad. I feel certain that many people who have died by suicide have put considerable thought, planning and precision into carrying out their final act. Which in my opinion takes a certain amount of intelligence and rationale (and that's what happened with you, my darling girl).

All of which has kept me wondering who has the bigger problem, given how in every suicide we all missed the signs that would indicate so many wonderful, brilliant, sophisticated, charming, funny, loving, giving, beautiful human beings were in trouble. Or at least, what those of us left behind perceive as trouble.

While I can admit you were depressed, my precious girl, and I so wanted you to not feel so unhappy, nothing else about you would indicate you were mentally unfit. At least, I don't want to think about you in this way.

Most of us are troubled and unhappy at some point in our lives. And while I would agree that the killing of one's self is not normal and I can understand why suicide suggests a mental imbalance of some kind, when it comes to the staggering numbers of children, teens and young adults dying across the globe, that's a lot of mental imbalance to consider. Adding in older adults dying by suicide that we don't even consider shocking, I have to ask: is there this much mental illness and imbalance in the world that everyone remains equally at risk of self-harm? Maybe because of one major trigger or a few piled up? What is going on?

I suffer from PTSD and depression as a result of losing you, my darling child: both defined as a mental health issue. But I'm not alone. Recent Canadian statistics show that seven to ten people are profoundly affected by one suicide. Adding these numbers to those who have died and are known to be at risk of suicide (not counting those who don't or can't reach out for help), this makes the number of individuals struggling with their mental health around the world almost incomprehensible.

Because of the tendency in western society (maybe everywhere in the world) to explain suicide as the result of a mental illness without exploring other potential reasons, I have always hesitated to accept mental illness as the only plausible reason, not only for your death sweet daughter, but the suicides of many people. There have to be other reasons to explain the shocking number of suicides worldwide. Are we all to blame in some way?

Of the suicides and attempts recorded, globally 800,000 plus people die by suicide each year. That is at least one person every forty seconds! At the same time, more than 20 others are attempting suicide. It is estimated that 160,000 of suicides are children, teens and young adults aged ten to twenty-four. The state of one's mental health on its own cannot be the only reason children, teens and adults of all ages are choosing to leave this planet by suicide. Is there something wrong with our society? Are we somehow failing each other in large numbers as part of both a local and global community?

Returning to stigma and those of us suffering the aftermath of a suicide, and knowing that suicide is the second leading cause of death for children and young people worldwide and on the rise, what is happening? Are we in the midst of a human crisis we don't understand? Should there really be any stigma associated with suicide anymore given the numbers of so many people both dying and impacted by it? Trying to survive? I don't think so. We're all at risk of some type of suffering related to suicide. This topic can no longer be ignored.

Looking at information online, mental health agencies state that no one knows why young people are killing themselves or what to do about it. Given this and as the bereaved parents of these young and beautiful souls leaving, what hope is there for any of us to forgive ourselves our perceived failures and let go of the shame we feel because we didn't do our job right? That we never protected our kids from themselves? I'm not blaming you for taking your life, my darling girl, but something went wrong somewhere.

Who is responsible for suicide anyway? Are children and youth as young as ten and to their mid-twenties, before their brains are even finished developing, mature enough to be held accountable for their death? Not that you could be. You're gone. But if as a society, we don't put suicide down to mental illness, we have to start looking elsewhere for the reasons so many of you are choosing to die. And if you're not to be held responsible, then who? Me? All parents? I certainly carry the guilt and shame from feeling at least partially responsible for your death.

If not the parents alone, does it boil down to the responsibility that all individuals who are involved with every child's life have, and that together, we all must pay better attention to the needs of our kids (every individual, really) in the midst of our eroding social conscience? Could it be that every one of our kids could have been saved with the right intervention? You can see the can of worms this represents if we were to have a proper discourse on the topic. It would throw that can wide open. In the meantime, and because we are not, our children just keep on dying.

If every child could have been saved from death at their own hand, this would have to have been from the insight all bereaved parents can only wish they'd had in looking back. Clarity comes quickly after our child dies. It's easy to see after the fact everything we wish we had known and could and should have done differently that could have potentially saved our child's life.

Ultimately, saving people from themselves requires that we know why they want to die. Part of this is understanding that they do. My biggest regret is that I didn't have more information about your mental health, sweet daughter, and how much at risk you were of doing harm to yourself. Of actually dying. All of which you faced alone. I will be forever heartbroken by this failure on my part.

I read long after you died that confronting individuals directly about their intention to end their life can sway that person to change their mind. Those surviving attempts have said this and were grateful later for the intervention. They turned their lives around. I like to think that if I'd known more before you died, I would have at least had the courage to talk to you about your mental health and any thoughts you had about killing yourself. I know you had them. I found out later.

I blame myself because I think I could have done a better job as your mom. While regrets are unique to every bereaved parent, I'm sure each of us would give just about anything to have the chance to do some things over again to try and keep our child alive.

Some might say thinking about your death in this way is too self-centered. It makes me seem more important than who I really am as only one individual. But as your mom and the one who shaped your beliefs about yourself (I thought you were perfect), how can I not help but think that I demanded too much of you? That I completely missed the part of you denying this and maybe even screaming out for help?

I couldn't see that you were in trouble (there I go with that word trouble again). At least, not as clearly as I can today. And, despite how many people have told me I am not to blame for your suicide, I am still filled with deep regret about this, too.

While I can accept that we all do the best we can with the knowledge we have, it is clear we *all* need to be better educated about suicide and the risk it poses to everyone, starting from an early age. Me not understanding why you would want to leave your family who loved you (and still does) and why you couldn't appreciate a world that though challenging, is not without its brighter moments, haunts me to this day. How I would have loved to share afternoon tea with you forever.

Then, I think about your brother and how well he's doing in life and think I must have got something right. For the good of my health, and because I can't go back and change anything, and regardless of how much I want us to be more socially educated and aware to save everyone from themselves, I have to consider that maybe your death wasn't about me. That anyone can be the best parent in the world and still lose their child to suicide, for whatever reason.

Most of us are scared of death. Since you died, I've struggled to understand what it is about the mind that one can truly just end their life. What it takes in that final moment to commit themselves to their final act on earth. In your case, what you were thinking. What made you want to die. Was it an act of faith that you were certain you were going somewhere better? That it was your time to go?

In my resulting agony, I could only see twenty-two years wiped out. Just like that! In minutes and from your own doing. I won't ever forget how shocking this felt.

When I attended a bereaved parent support group and witnessed the pain of other bereaved parents, many who had been grieving for years, I felt just a little that I didn't belong with them because their child hadn't chosen to die. Their child hadn't consciously chosen to put their parents through so much suffering (I know, it sounds a bit like I am blaming you). The only time I didn't feel so alone and as though something was wrong with *me* because *you* had chosen to die, was when another parent attended a session the same evening as I did who had just lost her son to suicide. This self-blame and shame often kept me from sharing things I felt about your death and my bereavement.

While I met many bereaved parents on dedicated suicide boards online, I found that their anger, pain, shame and embarrassment that had stemmed from their child's suicide kept them from wanting to bond with others, despite the fact we had all experienced the same loss. This was disappointing to me, but it's easy to see looking back that nobody knows what they are feeling, much less doing in the early trauma and grief. What is there to say, except to repeat the story of the death over and over? In order to bond and heal, you have to find people who are willing to explore and share their emotions and grief experience and want to recover from it.

Surviving the suicide of a child with other parents grieving the suicide of their child is unique and special. There are still plenty of people in general in the world who think that suicide is wrong, if not evil. That our children are going to hell because they took their own life. While I love and respect all grieving parents and know that we share many of the same feelings and pain in grief, I have a special place in my heart for those who have lost their child to suicide and are trying to survive without the support that is badly needed and specific to our recovery.

I would be remiss if I didn't say I also have a special place in my heart for sibling survivors of suicide. Imagine how shocking and insensible it seems to younger children and teens of siblings who choose to die? What the death of the sibling they adored does to them?

Many children hide their pain from their sibling's death to not worry and cause their parents further pain. We tend to idolize our lost child. Many surviving children believe they should have been the one to die instead of their brother or sister as they witness the endless agony of their parents (your brother actually said this to me right after you died). We couldn't find support to help him with his trauma and grief and the stigma he may face because of your suicide. It takes a strong kid to pull themselves through their worst pain without support and not getting into serious trouble, having to depend on parents who are emotionally absent. At least for a time.

You see what a mess of grief we are all left with when you kids die? Still, I will not make you wrong for going. Only wish that things had turned out so differently to how they did.

If I knew then what I know now, I would tell newly bereaved parents that while suicide is talked about more openly than in 2005 when my daughter died, it's still within a limited context. While national strategies have been developed in some countries to try and find ways to end suicide, looking at global statistics, clearly, they aren't working. As of 2016 and according to the World Health Organization data, only three Caribbean islands reported zero suicides of people up to age twenty-nine years old: one of them an island where I got married three decades ago. Our wedding song was the island favourite. *Don't worry, be happy.* And everybody there was. I wonder, elsewhere are we all just so miserable as a majority that we have forgotten how to be happy? How to treat each other with kindness and respect? How to care about each other? Are we equating happiness with all the wrong things?

While the 800,000 plus people dying every year by suicide may not reflect the majority of society struggling to such a degree they don't want to live, it is worthwhile remembering that the seven to ten people affected by every one of those deaths can create the same kind of emotional pain that those dying feel. As far as I know there are no statistics on how many parents die after the death of their child with the causes and manner of death broken down. But I can say that the feeling a parent can experience to join their deceased child can be compelling.

It's hard to find anyone who hasn't been affected by a suicide. They either have directly or know someone who has. Which makes all of us part of a problem we have yet to fully understand and fix. Or at least, try to fix.

While no one knows the true state of mind of any person who has died by suicide, it's a safe bet to say that they were suffering in some way. Maybe they were disillusioned with life. Maybe they were experiencing heartache or facing a problem they couldn't see as solvable. Perhaps they lacked purpose and motivation and couldn't see their way out. Maybe they felt like they never fit it and certain they never would. Maybe they thought they were unlovable, unworthy of love and that nobody cared about them. Maybe they were too scared to ask for help because they felt unheard. Misunderstood. Convinced they were a burden. Certain they wouldn't be missed. In short, they believed they were of NO value to themselves or anyone else. (By the way, much of grief can make you feel this way.)

For those reading this and you are worried about one of your surviving children or know someone worried about their child who is demonstrating feelings or behavior related to some or all of the above, it is critical that parents talk to that child. Get them to a doctor or therapist. Challenge their thoughts and intentions. One of the most important suicide prevention strategies is to directly ask the person at risk whether they intend to kill themselves. They may lie in their response, but at least you asked and let them know you care and are worried for their safety.

Because of the pain surviving children experience from the loss of someone so important to them, I can't stress enough how important it is that newly bereaved parents reassure their surviving children that they love them and are in their life for the long haul. That they can and will support them through whatever they feel challenged by, no matter what and regardless of their grief.

I'm not a doctor or researcher who has studied suicide. I'm a mom who lost her beloved child to suicide probably for most, if not all of the reasons listed above. And for any parent experiencing the same, it does qualify us to speak and share what we have learned to educate others, which can help us heal. Medical professionals have always been interested in hearing about my experience to further understand it.

While I can't go back to try and get my child help for any of the now obvious problems she was experiencing, and the same is true for countless other parents, those with surviving children or know someone worried about their child, should trust their instincts. If they are worried, it's for a reason.

Being aware of even just one sign that may be indicative of suicidal ideation I am certain, can save any child's life. Much more education is needed though, about how as a community of people entrusted to the care and development of our young people, we should be talking to them about suicide in all of their environments (family, learning, work, social, spiritual, religious) and in a way that never makes any one of them wrong for feeling the way they do. I absolutely believe this can help to instill compassion and caring within each and every one of them starting at an appropriate age, to feel kindness and respect for each other.

Two months before my daughter's death, she began to tie up loose ends that I took as a sign of her growing up. She was twenty-two. Some of the statements she made, though I thought them odd, I shrugged off. When she thanked me one day for being such a great mom, I thought it was a sign of her evolving maturity. I was really looking forward to seeing her develop into even more of the daughter and best friend she already was.

The last time I saw her, the day before she died, I took her grocery shopping. My husband and son were running errands. While we waited for them to return, we went for tea. I thought she looked and had been acting a little strange. She wanted only the type of food her boyfriend could eat. She wouldn't remove her sunglasses indoors. She was abnormally quiet. Stand-offish even. I felt alarm but shrugged this off as excessive and unnecessary worry because I couldn't put my finger on what I was worried about.

When we dropped her off at her apartment, we hugged. Everyone said I love you and we drove off. Within seconds we got a call from her, telling us we had mixed up an item. We circled around, made the exchange and said our goodbyes once more. A minute or so later, she called again. We needed to exchange yet another item. Laughing, we circled around, made the exchange, said our I love you and goodbyes and drove off again. It was the last time we saw her alive.

Though I spoke with my daughter on the phone the next morning, it wasn't a great call. She was desperate (my words) for rent money. I was trying to see the stuff she was made of to make it on her own, so I gently told her no. We couldn't keep bailing her out. Though I never said anything to her on the call, I decided immediately after that we would give it just one day and tell her the next that we'd give her what she needed. I never got the chance. She died that day. I don't know what time. Maybe right after we hung up. My calls to her that afternoon to see how she was doing went unanswered. Which haunts me to this day. I don't think I'll ever recover from the guilt I feel from the way that call went.

I am certain all parents who have lost their child to suicide replay their last days, hours, minutes and seconds with their child in their head too. I am also certain it is something many of them can't get over either.

For all of us going through the pain of losing our child to suicide, it is essential we not be too hard on ourselves. Having said this, as many bereaved parents before me have found and many will discover, this is a daily battle. We must be gentle with ourselves and as much as we can, forgive ourselves our perceived transgressions. It can ease the pain just a little.

I learned the hard way that my daughter was way more than what I ever could have dreamed for her. Back then, I was caught up wanting the most for her. A great education and career. What she really needed was for me to pick up on the cues she was sending that this wasn't what she wanted. While I'll never know for certain what she did, though she never said a word to us, her best friend told us she wanted to move back home because she didn't think she could make it on her own.

My daughter didn't directly ask us for help because she didn't want to burden us (her best friend told me this as well after her death). If we'd known she wanted to move back home, we would have brought her back in a heartbeat. It wasn't about the money (we had supported her financially to this point). She felt vulnerable and decided that she probably couldn't ever make it on her own. I was shocked by this revelation. I thought because we were close, my daughter knew we'd be there for her. I trusted she knew she could tell me anything. I was wrong. Every one of us who loved her were wrong in whatever way we thought we knew her. I've never gotten over this either.

Because those who plan to kill themselves often keep their thoughts private or they may swear just one trusted friend to secrecy, it is really hard for parents and others in their life to gauge when or if their child is in trouble, never mind being at risk of suicide. Most parents won't let their mind go there. It's only when it becomes apparent that we have failed to protect our child that we can feel stigmatized, believing we possess an obvious and disastrous character flaw. Fair or not, it's common to feel marked as an inferior parent and human being when your child ends up dead by their own hand.

I've long wanted to do my part to help increase parental awareness about the risk of suicide in all young people and help bereaved parents recover in whatever way they can from the trauma and grief trying to survive their child's suicide. I have found grief to be debilitating; the suffering severe. It can incapacitate survivors to the point of losing just about everything. As a result of this, we have struggled as a family over the years in many different ways.

Suicide awareness is not just for some people, but everyone. Anyone can be impacted by a suicide in a single moment. The irony is that survivors of suicide deaths need just as much help and support in their grief as those who have died should have had, too. As the one left behind and grieving, it is easy to inherit many of the same struggles as the one who has died.

We're all in this together. We all need to be kind to each other. Patient, respectful, caring, considerate, loving, compassionate, empathetic and above all, mindful of the fact that no one knows if or when they'll be the next to need help.

For information about suicidal ideation and suicide statistics, please see "Suicidal Ideation" and "Suicide Statistics" under Resources at the back of this book.

Survival

Survival is the act or fact of surviving (literally *remaining alive* after the death of someone or the cessation of something) under adverse or unusual circumstances. The death of a child is both unusual and adverse in every way imaginable. It is the least favourable circumstance to be in. The many things we must do to survive our child's suicide can make us feel like we have been immersed in antagonistic environments as we feel the need to guard ourselves against anything that feels threatening. For many of us, this is just about everything in early grief.

I lived for years, sweet daughter, *only* surviving your death. The family environment felt hostile and combative. Only after many months and when the initial shock wore off, the worst of the nightmares calmed down, and I no longer stared at the phone waiting for you to call or at the front door wishing you would walk through it once more, did I resign myself to the fact that you weren't coming back. From then on, every breath I took was to survive just one more minute of every hour of the agonizing twenty-four that was now my life. My inner and outer worlds had been totally devastated from your suicide. Everything around me was still way too confusing and overwhelming for me to try and make sense of in this new and horrendous world I did NOT want to be part of.

Through all the tears, whether I was focused on finding answers for your suicide or fixing the many problems that had engulfed our family, in reality, all of my efforts were the result of me trying to find a reason to stay alive. To survive. That much became apparent ten years later when I collapsed.

Survival at its most destructive is when you are literally trying to stay alive while feeling under constant threat. It takes a lot of energy trying to dodge every potential crisis. The acute stress we experience when faced with threat is from the adrenaline our body releases to warn us of impending danger. In this heightened state, our heart rate increases. Our blood pressure rises. We experience rapid breathing, body rigidity or collapse in the instinct to fight, freeze, flee or submit. Emotionally we are ramped up by fear, rage, anger and are defensive.

Any parent trying to survive the suicide of their child without understanding the trauma they have been subjected to will react to any potentially threatening situation with an instinct to survive. The same as early cave dwellers who had to remain alert at all times to the beast in the forest that threatened their survival at every turn. In trauma from grief, the beast we fight is the fear we feel about whatever may be lurking in every hidden space that could threaten us with something worse than what we are already experiencing after losing our child.

For trauma survivors, the survival instinct is the same as millennia ago. The only difference is that today, we don't usually go out and kill the beast. Instead, our hypervigilance that alerts us to real or potential threat produces different reactions in grief. In my experience (not a medical diagnosis), I'd offer the following as some examples of situations and behaviors in which bereaved parents may instinctually react to survive their loss and pain. These are:

1. Fight Instinct
Grievers with the fight instinct will react to their child's death and life circumstances in any number of combative ways. They

may act aggressively to try and find answers for their child's death and are determined to make someone pay. They may initiate legal proceedings and become involved in long drawn out court cases, for example in the case of an accident of some kind. They may fight for a change in law or become embroiled in another cause for change in remembrance of their child. While all of these are noble and needed, when they are driven only by the combative energy of an individual, it can leave the parent feeling depleted and empty if they feel they have nothing left to fight for. On a personal level, bereaved parents may turn to combative behavior dealing with relationship, family and other types of conflict in their life that can quickly ensure their circumstances remain difficult when only anger is driving them.

2. Flight Instinct
Grievers will try anything to avoid everything that reminds them of their loss. They want to run from their problems. They may move, quit jobs, leave relationships or act in any other number of ways that makes them believe they are immune to or over their loss. They may take down all of the pictures they had of their child, clean out their bedroom (if the child lived at home) and never speak their child's name again. In the case of suicide, they may lie to themselves and others about their child's cause and manner of death. In whatever way they behave, parents with the flight instinct do not want to accept, face or deal with their own, their partner's or any other family member's loss and grief.

3. Freeze Instinct
Grieving parents will partially withdraw or completely isolate themselves from others emotionally and physically. They will feel frozen in time. They may make their child's bedroom, or parts of their home a shrine in memory of their lost child. They

will feel stuck, frustrated, confused, directionless and frightened. They avoid making decisions. They may numb themselves to their pain in various ways. They may become ill and/or incapacitated in some way.

4. Submit Instinct

With submission, while in general terms this will describe the trauma survivor who ultimately submits to their abuser or trauma experience, with trauma from child loss, I'd suggest we submit to our grief when we finally collapse. It is at this point the grieving parent may find they simply can do nothing else but face their life with brutal honesty. Despite how hard it may be, collapse in any form gives the bereaved a chance to authentically assess their life and find in this the renewed purpose to rebuild.

Any psychologist or psychiatrist will tell you that the survival instinct is necessary even today to warn us of danger (not that we could do anything to change the way our brain functions). But equally true, our brain is designed to return us to normal functioning when the danger passes and our fear subsides, which for most people under normal circumstances, it does. Traumatized individuals become trapped in survival instinct when their fear system hasn't reset to normal. This causes them to remain hypervigilant to everything that they perceive as dangerous, which after losing a child to suicide can be anything and react instinctually to survive in this new and upside-down world.

I know for a fact that surviving takes a lot of energy. The stress alone from only trying to survive life can cause debilitating illness and upset. Irrational and chaotic thinking can ruin relationships and so much more. As an example, and getting back to you, my darling girl, I remember being frightened to death for years that your brother would die too, even when he crossed our yard to visit his friend next door. I worried he would be attacked by a wild animal (remember, we lived in the country?) or die some other way whenever he was not within my sight. I still worry he may die, though not to the same extent I once did.

Because of the trauma I experienced from losing you, I have been left with the instinct *only* to survive. It has become a force to be reckoned with in the suffering I've experienced and that I am certain all bereaved parents experience when they have lost their child. I have concluded, at least for those of us who have been traumatized from losing our child to suicide, we have become trapped in fear largely because we never can know the reason for your death. That the same hurt or worse could shockingly befall us at any moment keeps us wary and on guard for anything that could bring more tragedy in our lives.

I believe that all bereaved parents live in survival mode, at least for a period of time, no matter how their child has died. I've met some who wanted to or did pick fights, flee and have felt frozen in their grief. Maybe those with the most pain on their faces had submitted to their pain long ago and allowed it to control them. In whatever way these parents were living their lives, all in my view, were doing so from the instinct only to survive (legal battles, relationship breakups, going away and leaving everything behind, wasting away from illness and despair). Since you died, sweet girl, I have managed to survive all that has befallen me in one way or another, never wavering from my obligation to stay behind. Many times, I just wanted to run away or curl up and die. Often, I had no clue what to do, so I did nothing. Always I felt used up and worn out until eventually, I collapsed.

At the time of my collapse, all that had fueled my survival was suddenly gone. There was nothing left inside to push me to keep going. Yet this collapse gave me the time and perspective I needed to understand what I had been through and now needed and wanted for my life. Eventually, I discovered this was the balance I could only achieve through the compassion I could finally feel for myself.

Looking back, I can see how damaging that only surviving has been to my health. For years, I was creating the exact opposite results to those I really needed and wanted in my life that we can only obtain when we are relaxing into life.

Though I still must strive to maintain balance in my daily life and without doubt I want to heal, I still question the degree to which I will be fully able to. The trauma I experienced and Post-Traumatic Stress Disorder I acquired has seriously impacted me. Research has shown that about a third of those with PTSD will not fully recover, despite their best efforts. Healing depends on the degree of stress and anxiety, along with other factors the traumatized person has experienced. Not insignificant is the fact that one's memory of their trauma can never be deleted. Science doesn't yet know how to factor this into healing. As such, all I can do is continue to make the best effort I can every day to manage my symptoms and my life and hope for the best possible outcome.

If I knew then what I know now, I would tell newly bereaved parents that much like the thoughts I shared on trauma and PTSD, the earlier one knows how quickly they can be thrown into survival mode from the shock and trauma of their child's death, the sooner they can reach out for help. It is essential they understand the difference between survival versus balanced living. In the first, they will react to everything around them from the instinct to survive. There is no clarity or planning for the present or the future. In the latter, they understand that choices can be made to solve problems using logic and planning to bring peace of mind.

Understanding this difference early on can help bereaved parents avoid conflict and complications that frequently arise after the death of a child.

To determine whether they are suffering from trauma after their child's suicide, bereaved parents can research trauma symptoms and see their doctor for a medical diagnosis where there is concern. Their doctor should be able to refer them to the proper resources for support. While I found support online and tools to manage some of my trauma symptoms on my own, healing from trauma itself must be done under the guidance of medical experts. However, whether or not a bereaved parent seeks treatment for trauma is their choice. It is essential in my view that grieving parents at least educate themselves about their health and any trauma-like symptoms to decide the type of support they need or want.

My intention in sharing this information is to alert newly bereaved parents to the risks of trauma and understand how it complicates grief. Having the goal to live more balanced in grief from child loss is one worthy of striving for. However, balance can only be achieved in steps and over time when we have a clear understanding of our overall health and what we need to heal at any given time.

There are no easy steps or a fast way through grief after losing a child. In fact, it can last a lifetime for any bereaved parent. That being said, I can emphatically state that healing can and does occur in various ways throughout our long-term suffering.

If I had to go back to my earliest grief, I would have wanted to know specifically about trauma. I would have wanted to understand the survival instinct to hopefully avoid many of the additional problems our family struggled with for years in our respective grief.

If more professionals had the knowledge and skills to treat trauma from child loss, every newly bereaved parent could get the help they need with their mental health right after losing their child. However, this support must come from professionals trained in treating trauma and where the treatment can be modified to help them recover from the unique experience of child loss. It would take a special kind of therapist because it produces a certain type of trauma.

I can't emphasize enough that there are solutions to every problem and different ways of doing life than what we believe is only possible in our suffering. Whether this is from the pressure we put on ourselves to be a certain way in grief or because we feel trapped by specific circumstances, it is essential to remember that solutions can be found for every problem. We can change life up.

It's important that newly bereaved parents remember that everything is fluid in grief because we change so much throughout it. While sometimes it is better to remain in certain circumstances because it's not the right time to make a change, even though we really want it, where there is the will there is a way. Change requires us to have courage and trust that we won't let ourselves down, whenever it is meant to happen.

Having said this, it is a fact that trauma diminishes many of our mental, emotional and physical capabilities. It makes us feel insecure to the point we believe we have to fight our way through life. Understanding what we are actually experiencing from trauma will help us regain the balance we so desperately need after losing our child, which helps us heal.

No matter how any parent ultimately copes with the loss of their child, it is important to remember that survival on its own can only take us so far. Whatever tragedy we have experienced, eventually we will be forced to face the truth of our experience and our pain. But in this revelation, also comes the opportunity to decide who we want to be. Healed or not, no matter how long it takes to get there.

Finally, I would tell newly bereaved parents to take their grief slow. There is no point trying to rush themselves through the process or beat themselves up if they aren't where they think they should be. There will be plenty of time to reinvent themselves.

Despite all the mistakes I may have made, and all I missed out on early in my grief, I don't regret anything I've done in my efforts to heal. I can appreciate it is the steps I've had to take, with and without certain knowledge at any one time, that have brought me right to where I am today.

I am grateful that after fifteen years of doing life one way, I have the ability to now do things differently. I feel stronger. I want more for my life. I can sense a little spark of who I once was bubbling below the surface wanting to come out, even though I now am very different.

Time has given me a new perspective. It's taught me to better discern my needs. I've put a stop to only surviving. I have more confidence to claim what I want and need. The same that will be true one day for everyone new to their bereavement.

Vulnerability

Oh, darling girl, what isn't there about your suicide that hasn't made me feel vulnerable in so many ways? I have been weakened in mind, body and spirit and have regularly succumbed to illness and upset on a whim. Like a soldier on a battlefield, feeling oh, so susceptible to being wounded by a word or action of a loved one that is almost always the result of their misunderstanding. Both of who I have become in pain and who they are in their own. The opposite is true for me, too. We are all so different now.

The anger and criticism, pressures and fear we all have felt from your death we have used against each other as weapons powerful enough to wound in many ways. Wounds I have accumulated and that for years, have kept hidden from everyone all the ways in which they've hurt me. What is the point of trying to make others understand the sorrow that I feel? It runs so deep I fear that it has weakened me to such a point, I have lost myself somewhere between my will only to survive and my sincere effort to get better.

Not wishing to be further hurt by any miscalculation on my part of the compassion someone has to fully understand my sorrow, I have become cautious in what I share with others. Hence, my rather lengthy confession to you, my darling girl, who I miss more than you could know. The pain I still feel from your passing can overwhelm me without a second's notice. It either forces me to close up tight or risk opening myself up to emotions I'd rather not feel. Still, I can't prevent them from overwhelming me.

It is these intense and unpredictable emotions that people fear. I did too, trying hard for years to hold the worst of my pain at bay because I thought it would destroy me. Yet here I am, brave enough to scour through every area of my life to try and see where I failed you. What led you to your death. Finding no one else to blame, I feel I must have been the reason things turned out the way they did. It makes me feel vulnerable just thinking about putting myself out there in the world as a mother of a child who chose not to live.

I know I am obsessed with this thinking and not convinced it will be easy for me to change. I also know it sounds like I expected you to live for me. And maybe I did. It seems I never was completely able to let you have your life.

Instantly on becoming your mom, I took my role as guardian of you very seriously, despite the obvious mistakes I made. It never crossed my mind that one day you'd be gone. Certainly not that you would take your life and not because of something I may have said or done. But now that it has happened, I must consider whether I failed you in any way and if so, what was it that I said or did?

I think it's natural I would blame myself entirely for your death. Despite giving you everything I thought would make you feel happy and secure, I was wrong. That I couldn't see how wrong I was will likely keep me doubting myself for years.

I've beaten myself up mentally and emotionally so often just thinking about the times I expected more from you than you could obviously handle. I feel terrible that I never completely understood you and saw too late how vulnerable you were. Instead, you fed my dreams.

Spiraling into my own depression after you died, I quickly saw how unlikely it was that without the understanding and compassion you deserved for whatever you were battling, you could ever have had your own dreams or even found the motivation to go on. I can see where life probably felt overwhelming for you, if you could feel anything at all. Is this what happened? Was it me or life itself that was too demanding? Was I just too blind to see?

I ask because this is how I've felt in my bereavement and how I often feel about others who cannot truly see me. Oh, for the chance to do my life with you in it, all again.

It is this constant searching for the truth that has diminished my sense of who I was before you died and who I am today. Not so much my ability to offer whatever good I can to the world, but to have a sense of pride about who I am and all of my accomplishments. There is this grey area in how I see myself when you were alive; when I could and should have been so much more, and after losing you, when I can now see all of what this was.

From my years in grief I know just how hard we can be on ourselves as bereaved parents, which can only last for so long before it breaks us down completely; into a shell of who we were. Yet, I can't seem to stop.

Not being able to accept that all of the events in my life are the reason I am here goes against all my beliefs that formed the foundation of my adult life. And, in every other area I can accept this. It's your death I can't accept. I really think it was my job and that I failed to keep you from all harm.

This inner battle with myself about whether this is true or not, I'm sure, has kept me from rising up to once again become the confident person I once was. Able to take on anything. Some days I care. Some days I don't. Sometimes I haven't got a clue what I am working for or where I'm headed. My life can seem without any real purpose. And, very lonely.

And then, I look for that little spot of brightness I know must be in some corner of my clouded mind (a sure sign the old me is in there somewhere). I am self-disciplined enough to know that wallowing too long in the darker parts isn't healthy. And in these moments, I also recognize it is likely time I turn that compassion I can so easily feel for others toward myself. To loving and accepting me for who I was before you died and who I am today *because* of all my flaws. Perhaps it is these that have helped me more than anything to survive and become stronger than I thought I ever could be.

If I knew then what I know now, I would tell newly bereaved parents to expect that they will criticize and punish themselves for years for all their failures. They will hold themselves hostage to the idea that they are responsible for their child's suicide. I'd be surprised if they didn't feel this way. While many people may be quick to tell them it wasn't their fault their child died and not to think this way or that, the truth is, bereaved parents may find, as I did, that not one person can truly convince them that they didn't play some role in their child choosing to die.

While I'm not suggesting this is true, they may find when looking deep within themselves that they will always feel at least partially to blame for their child's suicide. Which is a horrible feeling to live with. As I discussed in *Suicide & Stigma*, on a larger scale I think we are all failing each other in society. I saw immediately after my daughter's suicide that no one was there for her the way she needed them to be. Her family included. This truth has haunted me for years.

For those who say the past is gone, we only have the future and there is nothing more that can be done (people do say these things), I'd reply that coping with the grief from losing a child is different. For many if not all bereaved parents, it's a years-long battle just to come to terms with the death of their child. I think this is especially true when the death is a suicide. Rather than fight further with themselves about what they could or should have done or the actual part they played in their child's death, it may be easier for bereaved parents to just accept what they believe and let it be. When I remove the pressure to rationalize my daughter's death in any way that feels wrong to me, even when I know it may be a healthier way to think, I instantly feel relief. Right or wrong, what we believe is our truth and the one *we* have to live with.

While clearly, no parent who has lost a child to suicide was able to save them for whatever reason, to compensate for our transgressions, we will punish ourselves just enough to ensure we keep suffering in some way. We are our own worst enemy, believing we weren't smart enough, quick enough or courageous enough to confront the glaring problems that we can see immediately after our child has died, were right in front of us all along. Hindsight, while it offers healing, also traps us in our pain.

We let beliefs go that no longer feel healthy *only* when we are ready to let them go. Unhealthy beliefs make us feel more vulnerable and open to attack. Whether this is from the beliefs we have about ourselves or how we feel we are being treated by society (people are still judgmental about suicide), until we know the reason why so many young people want to die, it's reasonable to think that bereaved parents will assume some, if not all responsibility for their child's death. I'm sure that all of us who have lost our kids believe we could have done a better job understanding our child's needs and making sure we did all we could to keep them alive. Sadly, hindsight can't save anyone already gone.

I would remind all bereaved parents that it is the compassion and gentleness they can feel for themselves in their vulnerability that will get them through the toughest times. Time will help them see and understand the truth of their experience.

Disappointment

As I sit here, darling girl; filled with words I need to pour out from my heart to clear my head of all the things your death has done to me, I feel great disappointment thinking about all the hopes and expectations I once had for you. For me. For our family. For all the wishing I've had to throw away about the way I wanted life to be. My disappointment that you went and died on me and dare I say, ruined all my dreams. For you. For me. For our family. No one has been the same since you left us.

I'm not blaming you for leaving. It's just that all my hopes and dreams were for our family as a unit. All of us *together*! Not apart. And, certainly not separated forever because one of us had died. Especially, not one of you kids. The thought of losing you to death never entered my mind.

So, sitting here, quietly contemplating that while loving them and feeling grateful for my loved ones who are here, I know for sure that the part of me that left with you: the part that held my dreams and wishes for us all has never been the same. It sits as empty as the day you left. I doubt I'll ever feel so confident again that no harm can or will befall any one of us still living.

If I'm being totally honest, I suppose I haven't thought too much about my disappointment because somehow, I feel that if I were to let it show, it may be construed by my living loved ones as proof that they aren't enough for me. That somehow, they don't matter because *you* were the glue that held me together. You were the one I loved the most. My struggle to accept your death may be evidence enough to suggest this, no matter how untrue it is.

I can assure them all that before your death, every family member played an equal role in filling me with all the love and contentment I enjoyed. It's just that your prolonged absence has made this rupture in the family feel so much more permanent with every passing year. Nothing can be done to fix this.

I wonder, do all bereaved parents feel like this? Stuck in time, trying to make sense of a single moment that caused so much damage to so many? Where nothing can be done to make it all seem right again?

Somehow, it feels wrong to feel disappointed about my life. There are others here who need my full-on love and attention. Maybe they are disappointed too?

I know that feeling disappointed is directly linked to my inability to feel excitement about anything because of my uncertainty that only good things will happen for me and those I love. My ability to anticipate only goodness and happiness for each of us remaining instantly left me when you died. To this day, I'm unable to completely trust there will be no further tragedy. All the sudden deaths since yours of those I loved, despite them all being from natural causes, have shown me that life cannot be trusted.

It's no wonder that I hesitate to plan too much or think that any dreams I now could make would not be crushed so quickly and completely by some further sorrow. Yet, if I could allow myself to have at least one wish, other than that you were here, it certainly would be that nobody else I love would die.

Feeling disappointed with my life and untrusting of the future is definitely not the best way to live. But, freeing myself from this one place that has me stuck in time is not so easy. You really were an intrinsic part of all that fastened me securely to the contentment and the love I felt before.

If I knew then what I know now, I would tell newly bereaved parents and those still struggling with the loss of their child from an earlier time, to remember just how devastating it is to have to give up on their hopes and dreams. Every parent has dreams. For themselves. For their children and their family. It's natural to feel disappointed when life has not turned out the way they thought it would.

The newly bereaved should know that reminders of how much they *have* lost will constantly assail them. This starts in early grief from the sympathy they receive from others who all will quickly return to the normalcy of their lives. Friends may drop away. Nothing will feel the same. They will find it difficult trying to put their own family back together again.

As newly bereaved parents, they will immediately feel how different they now are from parents who are not bereaved simply from the reaction they get when people hear about their great misfortune. They have instantly become every non-bereaved parent's worst nightmare. The person no one wants to be. For people who stay away or back off, it's as though not knowing too much about child loss, if anything at all, will protect them from the same fate.

People still shriek in horror when they find out my daughter died (often I don't even mention suicide). This reaction to child loss is typical and never goes away. It makes the grief cumbersome and isolating for parents who do want to talk about their lost child.

In trying to manage their disappointment, regardless of what they may feel disappointed about, the first thing newly bereaved parents must come to terms with is understanding that what they dreamed and expected for their lost child and their family that included them can NEVER happen. How long it takes to let their dreams and expectations go will be different for every bereaved parent. But they must at some point, let them go.

Letting go requires severing ties to the past and being able to reconcile themselves to their new life without their child. This is an extremely painful process that can take years and that no bereaved parent *wants* to go through. However, it is an essential part of healing.

Losing a child instantly changes everything for everyone who was close to that child. While grief impacts parents and siblings the hardest, and newly bereaved parents will likely find the devastation they feel from their child's death will be unequalled to anything else they've experienced in their life, it's important they remember that grief also affects grandparents, other extended family members, the child's friends and even friends of the family. Altogether, the grief from child loss leaves in its wake chaos and destruction that everyone must wade through in their own way and time. What one ultimately endures in grief will depend on their relationship to the child who has died and how the loss has affected them.

It is essential grieving parents remember that nobody will grieve like them. When they see family and friends moving on with their lives, it can hurt. They should remember this is normal and to be expected. However, because feelings and emotions are complicated for bereaved parents, should they perceive the grief of other people as disingenuous, it will create conflict and can even end relationships. It is imperative newly bereaved parents remember no one else *can* grieve their child in the same way as them. Nonetheless, other people will grieve their child and have a right to feel whatever pain they feel from the loss.

I was somewhat possessive of the pain I felt from losing my daughter for many years. I did not believe anyone else could love my daughter as much as me or feel an inkling of what I was feeling. While most likely this was true, it caused me to feel resentment towards others if I believed they were feeling too much or not enough grief. Time has helped me soften my views on this and give up the resentment.

While I agree with every bereaved parent who has said that living without their child does not get any easier, not wanting to sound altogether without hope for those new to grief, I believe that the more we allow ourselves to heal, the more we can change how we view our loss. Still, I am under no illusion how difficult this effort can be, as demonstrated throughout these pages.

In my earliest grief, I was absolutely terrified thinking about how I was going to manage the rest of my life without my daughter. I read every book I could written by a bereaved parent (less than a handful) to try and find the secret to survive my child's death. There wasn't one. In fact, no one had anything to share other than their own story of loss and endless pain. Every parent believed that things would get easier the more time passed. All of them said it didn't. Which left me feeling hopeless and even more depressed wondering how I could ever live my life free of pain.

Today, and wanting to encourage every newly bereaved parent who is feeling the same way in their early grief: terrified from what life has thrown at them and wondering how they'll get through the suffering, to remember that every effort they make to do anything should be viewed as a victory. Initially, this may be only to get out of bed, move their body, take care of their surviving children, look after their pets or tend the garden. Eventually, this may include a return to work or socializing a little. Added up, every single effort will lead them to their life getting better, though for most if not every bereaved parent, this will be a long road to recovery.

I doubt I'll ever get over my daughter's death. Deep down, I'm not even sure I can. The pain from child loss runs deep. The triggers from trauma frequently take us by surprise: such as facing our child's death anniversary and their birthday. The holidays. Watching surviving children grow and celebrating the milestones while drowning in nostalgia. Loving and hating every photo that remains unchanged of our deceased child. These are just a few of the triggers that never go away. How could they?

To this day, every time I see a family untouched by tragedy, I think how lucky they are. They still have the faces of dreamers. I'm far less envious now. Instead, I can feel happy for them that they still have their dreams to hold onto.

For those of us without this great good fortune (and here I cannot speak to those without surviving children), I wonder if perhaps the greater part of letting go of disappointment comes when we can shift our focus from the tattered ruins of what once was the fabric of our life, to the pieces of our family that have been stitched back together. To appreciate how blessed we are to have the love of them and all the contentment that this brings.

Shame

Shame is deeply associated with the social stigma of suicide that we must bear, but also relates to our own moral dilemma about what we believe is true about ourselves when it has been made so appallingly clear, that we failed our child. They died! By choice! By their own hand! What in the world does this say about us as parents? As decent human beings? About our capabilities? About how we can and should go about the world without feeling so much as even a slight stain upon our character?

While I'm sure none of us as bereaved parents sit around contemplating our shame, we don't have to. It hides in our darkness, reinforcing our core belief that we aren't good enough in some way. Certainly not as parents! We think of ourselves as inept. Stupid. Careless. Irresponsible.

The more we are affected by trauma and grief, and the more we see our interests and relationships deteriorate, the more we question ourselves about what we can do. What we are good for. Why we are still here. It can be a quick slide down the rabbit hole into the nothingness of despair.

My darling daughter, I want you to know I took my role seriously as your mom and guardian from the moment of your birth. Of course, like millions of other parents I had no idea what I was doing, but as time went on, I know for certain looking back that I only had your best interests at heart. I intended to keep you safe and made every effort to do so.

That you up and died on me has forced me to hide from others what I now really feel about myself. How I think about my failures. I wonder sometimes what people really think of me when they learn I had a child who killed herself. Maybe they don't think anything at all, but this is not the point. What matters is, it's *my* thoughts eating away at me. Nobody else's. I wonder too, what all this angst is doing to me long-term. It can't be good.

I've put on such a brave face for so many years, I fear it has become a lasting, though wholly inauthentic part of me. Which in itself is a shame, given I know in my heart how decent a human being I really am. I just made mistakes. Like everyone makes mistakes. I'm not sure any one of us as parents who have lost our child to suicide could pinpoint exactly where everything went off the rails. Believe me, I've tried. I'm sure they have too.

Every now and then, when I am chatting with other parents about how great our children are doing, I hesitate to give myself too much credit for being such a wonderful mom. Only the fact your brother is doing so well (though I'm not entirely certain your death and my grief hasn't harmed him in some way) saves me from the extreme emotional and mental lashing I used to suffer thanks to my harsh inner critic.

Any shame I feel is not about you. It's about me still needing in some way to take full responsibility for your death. I've always believed that as parents, we have been entrusted with the care and well-being of our children to the end of time. All parents and for those of us bereaved who still have living children know our job never ends. That our guidance is relied upon throughout all stages of our child's life. That our kids never stop striving to win our approval. We love it. They love it. Emotionally, it's a win for all, at least in healthy parent and child relationships.

To lose a child under our care *by their own choice and hand* naturally makes us, as parents, feel great shame. At its worst, shame forces us to hide the worst of our defects from others and endure the grating criticism we feel for ourselves from our core belief we are no good. That we are worthless, no matter how others see us. That we are bad parents. Somewhere, things went gravely wrong under our watch. We did not recognize our child was in trouble. We did not get them the help they needed to keep them alive (though no one, in my view, can truly blame a parent for not suspecting their child is going to die).

There is a *lot* of self-loathing and guilt to cope with for every parent who feels responsible for their child's suicide. The lasting pain is driven by the *choice* our child made to die without ever knowing why.

To this day, sweet girl, I cannot fathom you not only *made* this choice to die, but actually *went through* with your decision! I don't often let myself linger on these thoughts because not only are they too painful to stir up, but I know I'll never be able to comprehend your choice and actions. It's a futile exercise for me to keep trying. Which leaves within me a gaping hole I cannot fill with anything other than my sorrow and regret at not being able to have seen you differently. To have understood you. To have done more to help you find whatever it was you needed to make you want to stay here.

In the first year after your death, when I sat in a support group with other bereaved parents who had lost their children to illness and accidents, I felt oddly out of place. I felt distinctly different from them because I'd had a child who chose to put her family through so much pain (I know you didn't realize the lasting impact your death would have on all of us). It took me years to get over whatever emotion I was struggling with that made me feel this ever so slight distinction between us.

Today, I understand it was my shame. That painful feeling that arises from knowing that something has occurred that was improper (or plain wrong), done by oneself or another.

I want to scream to the world that what you did was wrong! That it was a huge betrayal of my trust for you that you would NEVER harm yourself. You told me so yourself. Once. When we were dancing around the topic in the most general of terms and never brought it up again.

My shame is not only about all that I've confided here, but the anger I still feel about you leaving me. I don't want to feel any anger where you may be the cause of it. Which is why it feels better for me to accept the blame for all that has transpired, despite knowing this is not the healthier way for me to think.

At some point, I am going to have to let something go if I am to rid myself of all this pain. Shame would be a good first place to start because of all the other negative emotions and false beliefs that stem from it. None of which are serving me any useful purpose.

I am a human who is learning. I am not a bad person or a terrible parent. I have to believe this if I am to believe everything else about myself that I like to think is good.

If I knew then what I know now, I would tell newly bereaved parents that most people are burdened by shame after suffering any type of trauma. Losing a child is a traumatic life event. It's normal to feel ashamed of their failures, whether these are real or perceived.

Shame requires time to understand and even more time to resolve because of the complex emotions stemming from it. Recent research into the more successful treatment of trauma, of which shame is a huge part, is changing the way many medical professionals are treating trauma survivors. The research has shown that therapists showing compassion for trauma survivors and in turn, helping them feel compassion for themselves, along with giving them the tools to help them regularly practice self-care, is a major contributor to their ability to attain optimal healing.

The ability to feel self-compassion normalizes the shame that many trauma survivors feel having experienced certain types of trauma. And in almost every type of traumatic experience, I'd agree that a survivor's ability to soothe their mind and body, given the many trauma triggers that can feel like a lifetime of assault, is healing. But I'd also suggest that bereaved parents may have to work a little harder and longer to give up the shame by convincing themselves their child's suicide was not their fault in some way. It's very hard to accept that our child was their own worst assailant.

To shift their thinking from negative thoughts about their self-worth to thoughts that reinforce their beliefs that they are valuable, worthwhile and loving human beings, it's essential that bereaved parents remember they are not alone in their experience. They are not alone in their shame and they never will be. There are countless parents in the world just like them battling many of the same things.

I would tell all bereaved parents on this healing path to remember it takes phenomenal courage to face their own worst self. But as they do, and as they become more open to new ways of thinking about their past, their child's death and their ongoing suffering, to trust that what they believe about themselves will change. So will their grief. More than just intellectually understanding their innate goodness, being able to really believe that they are fundamentally good, loving and decent human beings who are worthy of love and capable of anything, will make a huge difference to what they experience in their healing.

Therapists who use therapy with a focus on compassion to treat trauma state that getting in touch with one's innocence before shame helps survivors heal. For bereaved parents, I'd recommend frequently studying a favorite photo of themselves at an innocent age to help them remember the true nature of their innocence; before they succumbed to all of the relentless self-punishment after their child's death from all of their real or perceived mistakes. This can help them find the willingness to eventually forgive and love themselves.

In terms of self-care, the benefits of a more balanced life will come as bereaved parents increasingly surround themselves with people who are supportive, and they engage only in activities that they enjoy and feel calming. To escape the cycles of negativity that can last for years and maybe will persist their entire life going forward, being able to mentally switch from thought patterns that feel punishing to ones that are more conducive to their healing will help them create more harmonious environments and relationships. While all of this takes time and practice, these are all goals worthy of achieving.

I've found in recent years that recovery is not about resisting or trying to manipulate what we think and feel in grief. Rather, it's developing the skills to integrate all of what we think, feel and experience in mind, body, spirit and soul in our pain, and gather the tools along the way that can help us recalibrate ourselves, accordingly. All of this must be done over time and in steps and in my experience, is dependent on what is going on in our lives and the changes we feel ready to embrace at any one time. This is the process of healing.

I'd tell every bereaved parent struggling with shame that to begin to develop self-compassion, it can be helpful to reinforce in their mind all of what they once hoped for themselves. For their child and their family as a devoted and loving parent, partner and thriving human being. To remember all that they did do to protect their child from all harm and couldn't possibly have known the true intentions of their child (suicide is usually the best kept secret). To understand that they weren't bad then and they aren't bad now.

Missing signs is part of being human. Everyone who has lost their child or anyone else they love to suicide missed all the signs. As bereaved parents, it can be comforting to remember that they aren't the first and won't be the last to lose a child to suicide, as painful a reality as this is.

We are all part of humanity that is rife with pain. Critical to healing from shame is for the one suffering to imagine what they would wish for their life after suffering. When they have let go the worst of their pain. A big ask, but worth thinking about.

As a last point, I would tell the newly bereaved to be mindful of their inner critic. Everyone has one. Not until I understood just how tough I was being on myself was I able to even begin contemplating what I really believed about my worthiness. About what I was or wasn't responsible for regarding my daughter's suicide.

While change never happens overnight, it does start from a change in the way we think. In early grief, I recommend grieving parents use positive imagery and affirmations of love and kindness for themselves as much as possible for two reasons:

1. To help manage the horrific memories and nightmares (they should seek trauma therapy where required).
2. To integrate the subconscious mind with the conscious mind.

Integrating love and kindness for themselves will help them go back into the world to tell a different story about who they are. About who they can and want to be with a more compassionate sense of self.

Below are examples of positive affirmations to help bereaved parents feel love, kindness and gentleness for themselves and others in their grief and healing:

May I feel at peace.
May I have the strength to see my way through every challenge.
May I hold kindness in my heart for myself.
May I hold forgiveness in my heart for myself.
May I hold love in my heart for myself.
May I hold kindness in my heart for others.
May I hold forgiveness in my heart for others.
May I hold love in my heart for others.

For information and online resources related to shame, please see "Shame" under Resources at the back of this book.

Fear

Oh, darling girl, since your death, what haven't I been afraid of? When you first died, it took enormous courage for me just to get out of bed each morning, knowing I would never see you again. *That* was a lot to deal with in every way imaginable. Now, years on, it is only in my desire to continue moving forward that I've found the will to face each new day. In all that I do, you are never far from my mind.

Fear is a distressing emotion. It can be felt as dread or horror and is aroused by the threat of real or imagined impending danger, pain or unpleasantness. Every trauma survivor knows fear well. Reliving our traumatic event over and over in the mind creates the perpetual state of fear we live in until our trauma can be healed; which is not entirely impossible with the right therapy and tools. But, for the bereaved parent, and thinking about my early grief to now, I'm still not entirely convinced any parent could every fully heal from the trauma of losing a child; especially where death is from suicide and they will never have the answers to the endless questions related to their child's choice to die. There can never be closure, except what we invent.

Separating the fear that we experience in trauma from the general fear everyone must deal with in life facing a variety of situations, I learned to manage these last ones over the years. The fear I faced in early grief having to do things I'd rather not or when I felt woefully inadequate to do the job; or having to take that first step to initiate some change in my life, I proved to myself over and over again that all fear could be mastered. It always proved worse in my head than in how events actually played out in real life.

While this may not sound like much to some, given a majority of people fear change and must battle their own feelings of inadequacy, losing you sweet girl plunged me into a world where I was terrified of everything, from the moment you left. Finding the courage to bring myself back from the sheer terror I felt for years, I'd say the changes in me have been phenomenal. I essentially had to relearn how to live without you.

Sitting here, I'm actually proud of all my accomplishments, though I admit I don't consider these nearly enough. It takes confidence to claim one's worth and value. In fact, the confidence and pride any bereaved parent can feel for what they have accomplished is deserving not only of their respect, but the respect of everyone. It's no small feat to have to pick yourself up after suffering one of the greatest losses, if not the greatest loss, of all.

Speaking about fear today, if I were to disclose my greatest one, it would be that upon my own demise, I were to discover how much time I wasted here on earth; unable to appreciate all that I experienced. I really do not want to die feeling ungrateful for a life that truly was worth living. All of it. Not only the parts of my life before you died. That would be a shame. I hate to think I'd have to do it all over again just to get my lessons.

It's been years since you died, and here I sit, still shaking my head. Unable to comprehend all that's happened. We are all still sorting through the aftermath of the damage left in the wake of your swift departure.

Though I have written elsewhere in these pages about gratitude and my desire to one day be able to fully accept your death, I also fear I may have allowed myself to be consumed by so many damaging thoughts and emotions related to just a few short moments that cannot ever be reversed. I'd like to think this doesn't sound too horrible, but there is that part of me that wants to let it all go so that I can move on with my life. But, I haven't yet, found a way to do this (maybe because I do think it's too horrible). It all still feels so complicated.

If I knew then what I know now, I would tell newly bereaved parents and speaking from personal experience, that there are two distinct categories of fear related to grief. The first is the fear that overtakes us the moment a parent learns their child has died. Not being able to trust the ground they walk on or that any of their surviving loved ones; especially their surviving children, will ever be safe again, is normal. As parents, we are all vulnerable to losing more than one child. I have met a few bereaved parents and read in the news about many others who have lost multiple children or their only child. So, the fear we could lose another child is normal.

Also, and no matter what the manner of their child's death was, many bereaved parents (myself included) fear it was their fault entirely or that they didn't do enough to prevent their child dying. The list is endless of the reasons that parents find to blame themselves. This too, is normal.

However, and over time, as bereaved parents see that their surviving family is safe, and as they reintroduce routine into their life again slowly but surely, their trust in things will return. The exception is when fear is trauma related.

While I wrote about *Trauma and Post-Traumatic Stress Disorder* elsewhere in these pages, it is important that bereaved parents understand trauma-related fear can be debilitating. It cannot easily be controlled or overcome given that it arises from physiological change in the brain. Fear from trauma can keep an individual anxious to the point of near collapse when they are triggered by certain memories or events. For example, not knowing where a surviving child is, the parent may become terrified that they too are dead (I still experience this to some degree today). They may become overwhelmed by everyday annoyances and challenges that everyone must deal with such as: tending to home and car repairs, paying bills, making business calls, going to the doctor or dentist, shopping, driving, decorating for the holidays, socializing, helping others.

Bigger problems such as trying to avoid relationship conflict or fix relationships that are breaking down completely, fixing financial problems, dealing with health issues or managing work pressures, can cause the traumatized person to think and behave so irrationally from the heightened anxiety it can take them to the point of actual collapse (this all happened to me). It is essential in my view that bereaved parents understand trauma and seek the medical intervention and ongoing support that is required.

Finally, I would tell every bereaved parent struggling in grief, to periodically stop and take a deep breath. To remember that in the end, there is nothing any of us can do about the past or change what could and should have been. It can become second nature to feel we have to race against the clock to get things done. To achieve something. Perhaps this has something to do with proving our worth to ourselves.

Whether newly bereaved or bereaved for longer, no parent who has lost their child should try and force themselves to make any change to their life they're not yet ready for. There will be many fears for the newly bereaved parent to tackle. With courage, they can and will confront what must be done to get themselves through all the agony and challenges.

Living as a bereaved parent is not easy. In fact, it's horrible. On an individual level, I've often thought about what could be worse than losing a beloved child.

Bereaved parents, just like people who are afflicted by a loss of limb, must learn to live in a new way with a major part of them missing. As a bereaved parent, how do you describe to those who haven't lost a child what missing a piece of your heart feels like? It is impossible for anyone to imagine who hasn't lost a piece of their own. Which makes learning how to live again as an enormously changed person that much more isolating and frightening.

Compassion

My darling daughter, though I have felt a great deal of sympathy from others for my bereavement from your death, sympathy is not the same as compassion. Sympathy is the feeling of harmony that exists between people who share the same or similar opinions and experiences.

People who have compassion, while they can feel deep sympathy and sorrow for the other person's misfortune, can also put themselves in the shoes of the person in pain. They have a strong desire to alleviate their suffering.

Feeling sympathy for one another in our pain, we take great comfort commiserating with each other and are quick to support each other through our various ordeals. We know what the other person is going through because likely we've been there ourselves or know we could experience the same one day. And this is true for almost every painful event of which humans will experience at least one, but probably more throughout their lifetime: such as; relationship breakups, divorce, illness, accidents, expected or the sudden death of loved ones from illness; job loss and financial troubles.

Losing a child is stratospherically different. Most people can't imagine it and will never go through the experience. They haven't got a clue what the grief is like and don't want to know. It's not possible for them to put themselves in the shoes of the bereaved parent.

I can still remember how I felt with every sympathy card we got (there are no compassion cards for sale). I hated every one of them. They all reminded me of just how much we'd lost with your abrupt departure from our lives. Sorry was the common theme in every card. Though today, I can appreciate the offering of kind words and gestures from those who haven't lost a child, they meant little to me at the time. Contrary to comforting me, they only served to further alienate me in my grief because of how different I now felt from everyone.

There is a major difference between repeatedly hearing how sorry people feel for us as bereaved parents than having someone really want to sit and talk with us to try and understand what losing our child has been like. To offer their assistance in concrete ways. For example, asking what they can specifically do to help. What else we need. Holding our hand. Giving us a hug. Listening. And this should not be limited to only the early days and weeks after the loss. Compassion from others is something that grieving parents will always need, along with the compassion they can feel within for their suffering.

Compassion, as it turns out, is now being recognized in the therapy world as an essential component of optimal healing. While its full effects on the mind and body are still unknown, research is showing that people suffering from trauma can benefit substantially from the compassion they can feel for themselves and from loved ones and others supporting them in their healing.

When I discovered this little gem of information it stopped me in my tracks. The reason for my ongoing suffering finally made sense to me. The self-compassion I could feel for myself and the compassion from others I so desperately needed to feel were the key pieces missing in part of all the efforts I was making to overcome my pain.

From medical professionals to employers, friends, colleagues, grief educators and support groups, it is essential that everyone in the grieving parent's life should have a well-developed understanding and feeling of compassion for them instead of instinctually wanting to run from them because they don't know how to be around a bereaved parent.

However, I'll admit that expecting others to feel compassion for my suffering or the suffering of any bereaved parent is perhaps not realistic. For them to do so would mean that everyone not bereaved from child loss must be able to imagine our pain and what it would feel like to be in our shoes. Which most people don't want to do. They simply cannot let their mind go there. I get it.

While we all can imagine and accept our aged parents dying and can easily sympathize and feel compassion for others when we've experienced this loss, there are some deaths that remain taboo or just plain too scary for people to contemplate. Child loss and suicide are two of them. Having said this, I can't help but think how much easier our journeys as bereaved parents and suicide survivors would be in a world where we all could feel compassion for ourselves and each other. Where no one was afraid of us or couldn't understand us as parents trying to survive unimaginable loss or deaths that are considered taboo. But we don't.

Research has shown that we don't know how to *truly* feel compassion for one other. I'd suggest this is at least partly because we have been culturally conditioned to feel sympathy for and even pity others going through the same or similar pain we have experienced. We share our stories to help ourselves get over our ordeals and move on. But we haven't done a very good job supporting each other through our more difficult suffering, which I've never understood. Not in my early grief and not today.

Putting aside for a moment the latest research and focus on compassion in the treatment of trauma that is proving beneficial for healing, from my long struggle and sometimes desperation to be understood, I now feel some relief knowing the problem isn't only me. A major factor contributing to anyone's inability to heal is the lack of compassion we feel for each other in general. While this is only half the missing equation, the other and critical half, is our inability to feel self-compassion that would benefit anyone in their recovery process.

Oh, my darling girl, to change all that I think and feel about myself, what would I have to give up choosing only to be kind and gentle with myself? Yet, what better gift could any bereaved parent give themselves?

Feeling self-compassion balances our emotions. I have experienced this as a softening in my sense of self. I've been less anxious and depressed. It has reduced the shame I've felt for my past actions and the need I have to ruminate. Feeling even the slightest compassion from others helps me feel better understood and not so alone.

Extending the same care and loving attitude to ourselves that we would naturally feel for anyone else in their suffering helps us becomes less self-critical. Less alone as we discover we aren't alone in whatever we are going through, even if it isn't exactly the same. It helps us acquire a better understanding of how important it is to love, forgive and accept ourselves if we are ever going to transform our experience of suffering into one that is gentle and more conducive to our healing.

If I knew then what I know now, I would tell newly bereaved parents that the earlier they become aware of how important self-compassion is to their healing, the less suffering they likely will endure. While it may be easier to feel compassion for others in their pain, the compassion they can feel for themselves should not be undervalued. Having said this, they should take this effort slowly. The tenderness they will feel for themselves can only emerge as they feel ready to release what is no longer serving them in their healing.

Techniques to help bereaved parents develop self-compassion (some that are cited from clinical resources at the back of this book) are:

1. Being aware of what they are feeling, and where and how this is manifesting in their body. (*This requires a few quiet moments being still with one's body.*)
2. Placing a hand on their heart and imagine opening it to make room for all of the tenderness they can feel for themselves in that moment. (*Stop and do this anytime throughout the day.*)
3. Reassuring themselves several times throughout each day that they are worthy of love and support.
4. Repeating positive affirmations. Examples include:
   I am now making room in my heart to feel compassion for myself and others.
   I am worthy of love.
   I am attracting support and compassion into every aspect of my healing.
   I feel loved and supported.
   I have only gentle and kind thoughts for myself and others.

Everything in grief from child loss takes time, including healing. It's like the grief adage: *one step forward, ten steps back.* Some goals may feel loftier than others. Some may never be reached. Others may change. All of what they do, as long as their intent is to heal, bereaved parents will be on their healing journey. Regardless of what this may look like to them or others.

I am an eternal optimist at heart. I never give up. I can look back at all my years in grief so far and state without doubt that everything I've done has led me right where I am today for a reason. While it has been my journey, it may be one where some of what I have experienced may be what countless others will or have experienced too. Which is my reason for sharing.

I would gently remind all bereaved parents that grief isn't a race. Getting through their stuff isn't a "have to" or a competition with themselves or anyone else. Healing will come from their desire to heal.

My discovery of the importance of compassion in healing occurred at the appropriate time for me, as I consider my own next steps in healing. While I'd like to think that every bereaved parent will choose to no longer suffer at some point, I don't know if this is true. I've met bereaved parents well into years of grief who had stuffed their pain away. They got on with life, but it was clear that they were still suffering in some way (some even told me so).

In my very early grief, I made a commitment to myself and to my daughter that I would do the best I could to ensure I would not suffer forever. I didn't think this would be fair to either of us. Today, and understanding how important it is to feel compassion for ourselves in order to optimally heal, strengthening this ability that is within me, is sure to take center stage going forward in my effort to let go of the grueling punishment I've inflicted on myself for long enough.

A big part of not being able to let my suffering go has been my fear of how this may change how I feel about my daughter and the love I have for her. Suffering the physical loss of her feels familiar. Comforting. It's felt right for many years. I haven't yet found what would feel right without it.

I would remind the newly bereaved that there are millions of people living with unbearable loss and trauma. Many may be struggling with the same issues and challenges shared throughout these pages. It doesn't have to be this way.

My one great hope is that every bereaved parent who can learn to feel compassion for themselves can touch just one other person to help them begin to feel this same compassion for themselves in their own suffering, too. Like a domino effect and though this does take time, we all could begin to not feel so alone and truly heal.

For information related to compassion, please see "Compassion" under Resources at the back of this book.

Courage

My dearest darling daughter, it is appropriate for me to talk about courage right after compassion, because compassion comes from only two things: caregiving and courage. Where compassion comes from the awareness of suffering and the desire one has to alleviate or end suffering altogether (the caregiving part), courage arises from the will and ability we have to face our pain and difficulties without fear.

Being present with our own suffering or someone else in theirs *takes courage*. If you've ever sat with a dying person or someone suffering unbearable pain, you may have found within you the natural instinct to comfort them. You may have felt a need to care for them or help them in another way to alleviate some small part of their suffering. Instead of running from them, maybe you wanted to embrace them or sit in silence with them, just holding their hand. It takes courage to show concern and care for the vulnerable. And it is this same courage and caregiving we need to demonstrate for and administer ourselves in our vulnerability, when we have the desire to put an end to our suffering.

In fact, it is courage that has driven me (and probably most everyone if they were to be honest with themselves) throughout most of my life. I could write here a list of experiences going back to childhood that gave me my most vulnerable start: the same experiences that helped me develop a sensitivity to the vulnerabilities of others. Instead, I'll go back only to the moment

I first learned you were to be born precious girl, and the instinct I immediately felt to love and protect you from all harm, forever. That I loved you even then, there is no doubt.

Like all new parents, when you were born, I loved you more than life itself, though I was terrified not knowing if what I was doing was right or wrong. From the moment you arrived and throughout your short life, I always found the courage to make decisions that I felt were best for you and for our family; hoping like heck that things would turn out in the end. And they always did. Almost.

Surviving your death, while instantly allowing me to feel compassion for others in a much deeper way, has years later also forced me to reflect on the self-care and compassion I have neglected to administer and feel for myself if I am to truly heal. I need to lighten up!

Truth be told, I've never needed courage more than now; all these years after your death to just keep going. To not give up, still not knowing the destination.

It's not just the loss of you sweet girl, so suddenly and unexpectedly, that prevents me from being able to feel so certain of the future or maybe even that anything great could ever happen again. It's the toll that's been taken on my mind and body from everything that's happened through the years that anyone in grief must endure. It has a way of stopping us in our tracks in countless ways and always without warning.

For me, and apart from the mental health struggles I share throughout these pages, it's not only this and my physical health that's taken a hit. With regard to the latter, nothing serious. Just nuisance illness that continues to remind me of all that's missing in my life. I certainly can't do all I once could. Given I have been this way for years, I question whether my health is something I can really change, given how much I've tried. But more than this, it's also my fluctuating level of desire and not knowing what I really want. Some days I think it's more or less of this or that. Which means I have to continually find the courage to force myself to live; not just survive. It really is annoying. I never used to be like this.

If there is a silver lining in this whole experience, it is that one almost has no choice but to live in the moment if they are to try and get the most from life. Which is different than being stuck in a particular frame of mind that is usually negative and a place in time, which is always painful. Knowing the difference gives us the courage to change what we no longer like about the experience.

If I knew then what I know now, and thinking about the long and difficult road ahead for parents newly bereaved, the first thing I'd want to do if meeting them is wrap my arms around them and give them a big hug (a virtual one will have to do). They may be surprised how good it feels to receive a warm embrace from those who have walked the path before them and can feel true compassion for them.

The next thing I'd want to do is share with them the truth of how grueling the grief will be. It is complex and a type of grief that no one wants to talk about, except in limited and closed circles. Trying to survive losing a child is not easy, but I would reassure everyone new to the path that they can trust themselves to find the courage to do what it takes to move through every challenge.

Sometimes, I've disliked having courage and of being seen by others as strong. Somehow, it feels like it is tying me to this struggle more than I want. There is the saying that we aren't given more in life than what we can handle. True or not, I respect all those who carry far greater burdens than do I. Part of my survival, I'm sure, has been because I've always remembered from my first weeks in grief that there are those who have experienced tragedy far greater than my family's own.

Having said this, there is a danger distancing ourselves from our pain and tragedy by only recognizing those who are suffering far worse things. It is helpful to remember that what is tragedy enough for those of us having lost just one child, is still far greater than what many people will ever have to experience. In this regard, we must have respect for and treat ourselves with tenderness throughout *all* of our bereavement.

I would tell newly bereaved parents or those still struggling to remember the importance of self-care. Its healing properties cannot be underestimated for the benefits they bring. Anyone grieving can become a better carer of others when they first know how to care for themselves.

I'd also tell newly bereaved parents that it takes courage to get through many things in grief. It takes courage to reach out and ask for help. It takes courage to be kind to others. It takes courage to be considerate of other people's feelings and to take the action necessary to minimize conflict. It takes courage to stay open to ideas because there is always something to learn. It takes courage to see our difficulties as a harbinger of change. It takes courage to make choices based on need and want and to respond to situations rather than react because there are solutions for every problem. It takes courage to trust. It takes courage to make an effort.

Finally, I would tell anyone on this path to remember it is an act of courage itself - perhaps the greatest act of all, to survive the loss of a child. For those of us who have experienced this loss from our child's suicide that is one of the most unimaginable circumstances to be thrust into, we can only aim to try and do our best.

These pages are filled with the complex emotions and challenges I've struggled with in my grief. While I am definitely better today than I was before and want to give other bereaved parents hope for healing, especially those recently bereaved, the pain from losing a child cannot and should not be sugar coated. The only way to move forward from the horrific circumstances we've found ourselves in, is to trudge through *all* of what we are experiencing.

Every suicide comes as a shock. As parents of children who have chosen to die, we are left pretty much on our own to struggle through the aftermath. While support for bereaved parents from their child's suicide may be different in other countries, in Canada and from my experience and recent online search, it is insufficient. While there are general support groups to support adults surviving suicide spread sparsely across the country, there is no dedicated support for parents of a child suicide and their surviving children. Nothing has changed from when my daughter died in 2005.

Because I've longed for all bereaved parents to feel more included in society and have more spaces to learn about other bereaved parents' experiences, I contribute to creating this change through my writing and online support. But we have a long way to go to educate the public in general about child loss and grief, which is necessary if we are to create better support for bereaved parents. Specifically, parents who have lost a child to suicide and their surviving, dependent children.

My vision of healing has always been where all of us who want to heal have found the courage and desire to live feeling mostly joy. Where we have the will and ability to love and give, receive and live beyond our wildest imagination. Sound great? While perhaps too lofty a goal, it's fun to think about and we can at least try.

Confusion

My darling girl, I think it's worth adding a few thoughts here about confusion. For, if there's anything I've felt the most certain about in my life since you died, it's the confusion I have felt more than anything else. It isn't often I've felt completely free of it because of one thing or another going on. Perhaps everyone feels like this, bereaved or not. I only know that I was much more certain about everything else before that fateful day you died. When life for all of us changed forever.

I could recall, if I were to choose to revisit fonder memories, the happiness I felt just thinking about our family before you died. My vision was clear about where we all were headed. While I hadn't yet realized some of my goals, my prime concern was to make sure we all were happy and felt fulfilled. My joy arose from each of you depending on me and you all being there for me. I never imagined a moment without any of you in my life.

Despite a break now and then from my responsibilities caring for the family 24/7, whenever I pursued various work opportunities, I always found my way back to you. Without regret. To be with you and your brother the majority of my time felt like a calling I didn't understand. While I sometimes felt frustrated that my journey to "find" myself was taking so long, losing you just a few short years later, instantly made me feel grateful and today relieved, thinking about all the years I did devote to you. I know

204 Lessons in Surviving Suicide

deep down I did my best, regardless of this nagging inner voice that likes to tell me otherwise.

When we feel confused, we can't distinguish between what feels right or wrong or good or bad in any moment, or longer period of time. Our thoughts are jumbled (all of which is common in trauma and grief). Any stability of thoughts and more positive emotions we may enjoy from time to time will instantly be disrupted by a sudden trigger or event that throws us off our game. Anyone living with prolonged grief can attest to this. Very often, it is the confusion we feel that forces us to constantly move the line by which we can measure our recovery, as we succumb to that one step ahead, ten steps back feeling. Repeatedly.

While balancing our thoughts and emotions can help to minimize confusion, situations will still arise to test and teach us, no matter what we've already endured. It's exhausting! I've found that taking the time to think about my challenges and putting a plan in place to solve them is key to eliminating much of the inner chaos. Having said this, it's also true that in our vulnerability, every challenge can seem colossal, no matter how minor it really is. Not wanting to deal with problems or make decisions is natural in grief; however unpractical this is. We all must make decisions to get ahead. Which is why it's imperative we find ways to bring calm into our grief as soon as possible so that we can learn to once again make decisions with some clarity.

Right after you died, sweet daughter, the confusion I felt was different from today. My life had been uprooted in every way; my mind filled with terrifying thoughts and images from the trauma of your suicide. I can see now why so many traumatized people struggle to keep going. I felt like a caged lioness desperate to find my little cub and thought I would go mad from all of the mental torture.

I think it was only by some miracle that I found the will to get up every day. I focused on just one thing I thought I could manage.

In those first few weeks, this was feeding the fish that were once yours, and then I'd sit and stare at them for hours, feeling alone in my agony.

Eventually, I did a little yoga to move my body that had become stiff with pain. I found a couple of online support chat boards on which I met a handful of people with whom I started to exchange daily emails. We all had just lost a child or close family member to suicide. We quickly became each other's lifesavers as we shared our innermost thoughts and fears and supported each other in our pain.

As time went on and to help manage the overwhelming thoughts and images in my mind, I separated my day into three parts: morning, afternoon and evening (this was a great strategy I learned from a bereaved dad). Waking up each day, I only had to think about how to survive a few hours at a time what were otherwise endless, bleak days (time seems to move slower in intense grief).

I have never before or since been through so much agony as in that first year of grief. I understand how pain like that can push anyone close to the edge of crazy. It is difficult to explain to anyone who hasn't experienced it. In isolation, it can be deadly.

Separate from trauma symptoms, feeling confused about everything is normal in the first year or more of grief related to child loss. What to do. Where to go. How to manage. In grief, the standard rule is that grievers should avoid making any major decisions for at least one year after the loss. There is a reason for this. It takes time to adjust to life without our loved one. Even in death that is expected (for example due to aging), the death of one's life partner can leave a vacuum in the survivor's life that drains their will to live. I'm certain that many people quickly follow their spouse into death for this reason.

Losing a child, I'd suggest the time period is much longer as the impact from the grief is more severe. Since your death, sweet daughter, I've lost my parents, your biological father (he was the last living link to you) and several extended family members. The pain hasn't come close to what I've experienced losing you, my girl. In fact, losing you first may have impeded my ability to grieve anyone else.

Losing a child is on a scale of loss all by itself. Despite how shocked we are by the deaths of our babes to young adults (this latter generally considered mid-twenties), I've always remembered that every death represents the loss of someone's child where a parent has been predeceased. I am certain that anyone who has lost their child at any age feels the same devastation as those of us who have lost children who are youthful. In fact, I just read about a grieving dad, who having just turned 100, spent the last few years pouring his grief into creating a public garden to memorialize his son who died in middle-age from an illness.

Returning to the younger ones who have left us, our kids aren't supposed to die before us. Plain and simple. When they do it creates confusion for everyone trying to understand death that just does not make any sense.

Confusion at its best is a sign of growth. It is natural to feel confused when we are ready for change, thinking about what we must leave behind and what may lie ahead. Everyone experiences this. However, in grief, we can eliminate much of this confusion when we are able to sort in our mind what would be easier and the most beneficial when it comes to taking the next steps. There will be many.

If I knew then what I know now, I would tell newly bereaved parents to expect to feel confused throughout all their grief. Grief is not easy to recover from and nor should it be. Truth be told,

I expect to always grieve the loss of my child in some way. Who wouldn't? But, therein, lies the dilemma of whether we can truly heal from the loss of our child.

I struggled for years resisting this notion that grief was something we get over. I had read about this in every book I bought on grief (except those written by bereaved parents) and in news stories covering devastating loss (parents weren't yet over their grief from an accident or the fire that killed all their children 3 days earlier). That sort of thing.

We are meant to get over grief because it has a time and dollar value. The dollar amount assigned by an employer for a defined number of days off work to grieve (or the threat of potential loss of income from any prolonged absence), forces many grieving parents back to work and resuming other activities they aren't close to being ready for. When we are away from friends too long or inactive in our various communities, there is the risk of feeling further isolated or losing out altogether. While the need to sort out bigger things in early grief and this period of isolation doesn't last forever, having to reintegrate into a world that hasn't stopped at all from prolonged absence or starting anything new can feel overwhelming. There's a lot of "fake it" moments in grief.

I've found that recovering from losing a child is difficult. I've always been perplexed by those who say that time heals all wounds. It doesn't. It may only appear that way for those who've packed away their pain. In reality, our suffering always catches up with us in one way or another. I found it best to deal with our pain head on for a better chance to heal.

Finally, I would tell newly bereaved parents that any confusion they can't sort out to leave for another day. One thing that's certain in grief: as long they are breathing there will always be another day to tackle anything that's challenging them.

Faith

I thought it important to include my thoughts on faith, darling girl, because without it, I'm not sure how anyone can get through the ordeals we all must face. Faith is the belief we have in something for which there is no proof. For many people, their faith is religious based, regardless that the reaction of many newly bereaved is to question or blame the death of a loved one on their God. Alternatively, they may accept their God has now reclaimed their loved one who is safe and at peace elsewhere. Believing this can bring great relief to those left behind.

With suicide, faith is tricky. No matter how much faith we have, how can anyone reconcile their God allowing their child to end their life? I grappled with this question for a long time, given my mix of early Christian values and later spiritual beliefs that together, became the foundation of my adult life. With the latter, accepting that your death was one that was in perfect timing with your life plan (otherwise why would God allow you to die?), while it did bring me a measure of peace, it also left me feeling angry. It is a topic that today, I still can only talk about in abstract terms.

I was raised a Christian and regularly attended Sunday school and church as a child. As I grew into adulthood, my beliefs about God expanded to include those that were spiritual and metaphysical based. At the center of this was my steadfast belief that we, as humans (and all living things), make up a small part of this greater power that gives us the opportunity to do wonderful things. To enjoy an abundant life. To trust that all things happen in divine timing. To accept that there are lessons in every experience and as we expand our consciousness, we move on. Beyond having a general fascination with why we are here and the afterlife, I had no reason to explore more deeply all that I believed in and was already practicing. I enjoyed my life. Our family's needs were always met in line with what we all envisioned.

This all changed instantly when you died, sweet girl. While I never once blamed God for your death, my beliefs were severely challenged, and I could not understand why God had let you die. Did God really need you that badly?

In my questioning of why you had to die, I was left floundering between two worlds. One, where my life was nothing but mental, emotional and physical torment and where there was no reasoning or order. The other, where I felt more at peace and though I didn't like it, I could accept that all that happened did make sense (though it also left me struggling to understand why I would ever put myself through so much suffering). As time passed, instead of letting pain completely overwhelm or maybe even end me, I decided to try to find a way to reconcile your death with my living in whatever state I finally would choose.

And, it is here I remain. Smack in the middle of these two worlds, years later. Not exactly stuck. Not even really questioning the reason that this life-altering experience has occurred. When I choose to view your death as one that has gifted me with lessons I could not otherwise have found, however hard this is to accept, my life makes sense (I cannot speak to the reasons you chose to leave). But my pain is real. It's a constant reminder of just how difficult and unrealistic it is to try and live with both feet off the ground.

In my escape into my spiritual world, there is reasoning and logic, but most importantly, comfort. Feeling I must find a compromise in what would be most beneficial in how I choose to view and experience my loss and healing, I am left with two important questions that no doubt, are tying me to suffering:

1. Can we really *choose* the state in which we *want* to exist when something *really bad* happens?
2. If yes, why is it so hard to choose a life that is free of all suffering?

When the foundation of our belief system has been challenged or completely knocked down, it leaves us feeling lost and without purpose. Trying to find the remaining pieces or rebuilding a foundation from scratch isn't easy. While I still believe in the principles of fate and free will, your death challenged my view of the natural order of the world and forced me to find a reason for our existence. I still haven't quite found my way back.

A decade after your death, I had to face the reality that I was suffering from the physical pain of grief. A period of disability forced me to reassess all areas of my life. No longer could I try to make sense of my loss and grief through only the spiritual lens. I had to now assess the physical damage done to me over the years that spiritual beliefs alone, could not fix.

Over a two-year period, while I valued all I was learning about the physical effects of my grief on my mind and body, I found that life without my faith and spiritual intervention could not allow me to evolve beyond anything much more than my pain. People don't have healing powers or all the answers. Many don't even have compassion. Healing can only come from within and in my experience, is far more powerful when we allow ourselves to be guided by something more.

We are not equipped as humans to deal with suffering on a scale that is difficult to understand. Whether experiencing firsthand the same suffering as someone else or simply trying to help someone in need, our reach is limited. As the sufferer, we need something *more* to help us move beyond the pain. Something that helps us trust there is something more we can move toward that is within our reach.

In general, faith gently pushes us to believe in becoming more than who we are and what we can do as limited human beings. Faith gives us knowledge and inner power through awareness. It pushes us to ask the tough questions and find answers that can help us overcome adversity. And while this may still be too simplistic an explanation for all of life because life isn't so straight forward, after years of contemplation and the healing gains I've made, relying on my faith has led me to find everything I need that's been essential for my healing to this point. That I continue to ask and ask again the questions that I do is because it is the only way to push myself beyond the confines of my current thinking.

If I knew then what I know now, though far be it from me to try and convince anyone to find or try to hold onto their faith because it is so personal, I'd tell the newly bereaved that faith is a powerful healing force for those who have it. It feels comforting. It brings us relief. Faith can get us through our toughest times.

Maybe faith is built in. Maybe it comes to some people like a lightning bolt from one experience. For others, maybe faith has arisen from the smallest amount of light getting through to them from the tiniest crack in their shell that forever changed their life. One thing is certain. Faith is something that cannot be stripped away from us when we are securely fastened to it.

I believe that the Christian influence from my childhood helped prepare me for the pain I'd face in later years. I remember in my early grief, pleading with God (and the angels) to help me find a way out of the darkness. Dealing with one challenge after another, my life had become a minefield of explosions going off all around me often without warning. My only respite from the madness was the comfort I felt turning inward to my faith, and to my belief that I would always be guided somewhere better, no matter how bad things got. And I was.

Relying on my faith shielded me from taking extreme or thoughtless action and making decisions I may later regret. In looking back, and opposed to before my child died, I have no regrets in how I've managed my life and my environments throughout my grief, though there isn't one day of it I'd ever want to revisit. The entire experience so far has been a struggle. The grief from child loss is a long, painful road. I feel great compassion for anyone starting their journey. I know what they're up against. So does every other grieving parent.

As bereaved parents, we don't always conduct ourselves in ways that are rational or to some people's liking. It's part of the experience. I would reassure those newer to the experience that time does bring perspective to all things.

I'd also tell them that faith, if they have it, will be required of them the remainder of their life. It will help them accept their bereavement and by looking for the silver lining in every painful situation - itself a form of faith, they can trust they will be led by that *something* they believe in to get through every struggle.

Abandonment

It may seem rather strange to talk about abandonment immediately after faith, yet there is this fear I have that more loved ones will die and leave me feeling so completely alone. Just like you did, precious girl. I still can't get over the shock just *hearing* about your death. I can remember every excruciating second of that call. Lord knows I do *not* want to go through pain like that again, despite the inevitability I will have to face more loss one day, unless I too, am gone.

Because I know just how final loss is from your passing and everyone else in the family who has gone, I'm constantly bracing myself for the next onslaught of grief; hoping like heck it will be loss I can more easily bear. Which it will be (unless I were to lose your brother) because I've felt no greater pain than losing you. My grief related to all other family deaths has paled in comparison.

I've thought a lot about how feeling abandoned from the death of a loved one ties us to our longing for our life to be different. We want that person to be alive! This feeling of being abandoned by them from their death cannot easily be reversed just by remembering happier times. Many people extending their sympathies to the grieving remind us that we still have our memories. Well, I'm not sure how quickly any bereaved parent can conjure up only pleasant memories of when their child was alive. I still struggle wanting to remember earlier times and all we had from the pain I feel knowing all that we have lost.

Pleasant memories are a sign we can accept the finality of our physical separation to our loved one gone. Longing is a sign of all we still cannot accept. And in this longing is our fear of being further abandoned by the death of other loved ones.

The death of you, sweet girl, and the deaths of other loved ones gone have shown me that my fear of further loss is real. I don't want to be left entirely on my own. It already feels lonely enough with you gone.

I know that overcoming this feeling of abandonment from your death must be resolved within me. I could be in the midst of a million people and still feel lonely (maybe all bereaved parents feel this way). But letting go means I must be ready to accept my life with you gone. I'm not sure I'm ready to do that. I still want you to be here.

As humans, we are by instinct tribal. We thrive feeling we are part of a community. We need to feel a connection to each other to help us feel that we belong and are loved and safe. A host of problems can result later in life when our basic needs have not been met as early as in utero. It has been well documented that babies and children reared without a secure and loving attachment to their parents or other guardians suffer from abandonment. As adults, they can't form stable relationships or establish positive connections to people. Not even to their closest loved ones.

The hurt from any real or feeling of abandonment can cause people to experience isolation and struggle with negative emotions. In my grief I've experienced these as anxiousness, rejection, anger, fear, confusion, helplessness, sadness and depression and probably a host of others. These are not easy to overcome when we already feel alone in our bereavement and we are lacking proper support.

It's hard enough to accept child loss from a manner of death that can be explained. We are culturally conditioned to think that suicide is wrong. The reasons for these deaths can never be explained, which I'd suggest is a major factor that makes talking about suicide so uncomfortable for most people. Yet, to have any of our life experiences dismissed as too uncomfortable to talk about is just another form of abandonment that many parents must live with in the aftermath of their child's suicide. To cope, it's natural many bereaved parents may feel the need to isolate themselves to protect themselves from any further hurt or rejection. I felt abandoned by everyone. Not just you, sweet girl.

It is imperative we have regard for one other with the awareness that we all have the same need to feel connected to each other, loved, valued and respected to reach our full potential. Just one of our basic needs not being met places us at risk of not being able to feel that we can pursue anything beyond what is required for our immediate survival.

If I knew then what I know now, I would tell anyone struggling with grief after losing their child that feeling like they've been abandoned, especially when their child has died from suicide, in my view is normal. It can take years, if not a lifetime to come to terms with the loss of a child from any manner of death. With suicide, as mentioned throughout these pages, it leaves many unanswered questions and a host of lingering problems from the guilt, regret and self-blame all parents struggle with.

The feeling of abandonment takes away from us the sense of belonging that is so important, and also linked to losing our sense of identity in complicated grief. After losing my daughter, I lost all sense of my identity for a number of reasons. She was my only daughter. I now only had one child. A son (I love him dearly). I lost all confidence and strength. I had no vision and no longer a will to live. It took me years to regain any real sense of self and I have to admit, I'm still working on this.

When you no longer know who you are or what you can do and where you belong, it's difficult to feel part of anything. The feeling of abandonment, betrayal and a lack of trust for others are wrapped up together. Without the right support, it is very difficult to combat these and other negative emotions and the actions they sometimes drive us to take.

It is important that newly bereaved parents are aware, it is not always where they think they'll get the most support that they actually will. It's natural to turn to immediate family members initially in grief for the support we all so desperately need. However, support requires that the one providing it has a solid understanding of what the other person is going through and needs.

In my very early grief, I made my most valuable connections with other newly bereaved parents online. Those new to grief may find that joining a support group in person or connecting with bereaved parents in a dedicated online community to be beneficial, at least for a time.

After many years of trying to find my place in the world after feeling so abandoned and losing my identity (it's been difficult not being able to even casually talk about my daughter with others), I am less concerned about fitting in, which was something that was important to me when I first became bereaved, than I now am, wanting to share experiences and ideas with others. We need robust and thoughtful discourse on child loss, suicide, sibling and family grief and a range of other topics that will help all of us navigate grief and heal after losing our child.

All deaths by suicide take us by surprise. It's no wonder that as survivors we feel lost and abandoned by those who have chosen to leave us. The acceptance of suicide without condoning it would help us dispense with the stigma that has silenced our voices and help those of us parents who have lost our child to feel more like we belong. It would also help to create the space for families, health, education, corporate and government communities to come together to research potential causes of suicide and understand its ramifications and put in place laws and policies to better manage risk and prevention, and provide more funding to better support those at risk and loved ones trying to survive the aftermath, where prevention methods have failed.

I don't think this is a big ask, especially given that suicide is now considered a global crisis. I can't imagine how many millions of people are suffering the aftermath of a suicide. It's not just parents. I am certain that every death by suicide leaves all of their loved ones feeling abandoned.

My hope in writing this book is to help others feel less alone and where they one day feel guided, find the courage to share their pain and struggles to help others on their path. I long to learn more about how parents are doing and the challenges they've faced twenty, thirty or more years after losing their child.

It is true that once bereaved, always bereaved. As such and at some point, every bereaved parent becomes that parent with more experience from their longer years in grief. We all have something to share. We all can be a guiding force.

Peace

Ah, peace. That elusive thing I crave, sweet daughter. That stillness within my soul that I'm sure will once again be mine when I can put an end to all these warring parts within me.

Sometimes I wonder, if I had been left to deal with my grief without all the problems and distractions, would I now feel any different? Would I be farther along in my healing? Would I feel more at peace?

I know. This sounds a lot like an alternate universe that could only exist in my mind. My guess is that not too many bereaved parents (if any) can escape the harshness of the grief and life itself that we experience after losing our child. It's not practical to think we can hide ourselves away from the pain and struggle that comes with trying to survive all that we've lost. Even if we could, I doubt that in the long run life would feel more peaceful. There will always be something challenging us that helps us learn and grow, regardless of how cliché this sounds.

It goes without saying that when my inner and outer world is calm, I do feel more at peace. I really enjoy this feeling. I have no desire to feel challenged by anything, anymore. Whether or not it's realistic to think I could feel inner peace all the time is debatable, but that is my goal.

Now that I am aware of how important it is to be surrounded by caring and compassionate people when we are trying to heal (where we naturally are inclined to respond to them the same way), it is my preferred way to live. There is a danger we can make too much up in our head when we are alone too long or uncommunicative with those who do surround us.

Despite knowing it's not wise to compare ourselves to anyone else in grief, I can't help but be curious about the experiences of other bereaved parents. Whenever I do happen to meet a parent who has lost a child and I assume that they are fine by what they may be saying, I start to think it's me that's made my grief more difficult. That there is something I'm just not getting that is preventing me from moving past my struggles. I've learned two important things:

1. Never assume.
2. There is no such thing as *fine* for any bereaved parent.

From my earliest grief, I learned from every bereaved parent that I met or read about in books, they tried to convince themselves they were okay. I did too, for years. In many situations and quite quickly after loss, we are forced to put on a brave face and mask what we are really feeling when we have to go to work, get the groceries and do whatever else we need to do to survive.

Trying to push our past away that includes our lost child is hard! To this day, and though I curtailed my socializing years ago, I still have to brace myself before meeting anyone or attending events where I feel I can't be myself. It's draining!

It also feels like I'm taking a big risk sharing my thoughts with you so publicly, sweet child. But I felt there was no other way to explore what I am really feeling, and maybe what other bereaved parents are feeling too. I see no other way to try and find this inner peace I crave than by knowing what I need to heal.

Thinking back to when you first died, I was desperate to connect with anyone who had been through this loss and suffering the same grief our family had been thrown into. I wanted them to tell me that one day, we would be okay. That we would survive this horrendous thing that had just happened and was tearing us apart. My struggle to survive wasn't only about me. It was about saving our family. About bringing peace into our lives.

In my desperate need to feel this connection, I discovered there weren't that many bereaved parents immediately available to meet. In fact, it's true that years later I still have found that bereaved parents don't want to talk too much, if at all, about their feelings. Books on grief in general that I read, while helpful to a point, missed the complex struggles I was dealing with from losing you and trying to survive your suicide. Likely many of the same issues that thousands of parents everyday who are being thrust into this world of grief from yet another child dying, are struggling with too.

While I would suggest that there are a few, but minor differences in the issues that we face as parents who have lost a child to suicide than parents whose child's death can be explained, the pain is no doubt the same. Yet, suicide survivors are a grief group of its own. As parents, we are different still from other surviving loved ones as we search to find the reason why our child chose to die. A search that can last years.

Hence, my candid sharing with you, my precious daughter, which I felt I could only do by speaking directly to you from my heart. This manner of communicating has helped me remove any filters I might otherwise have placed on my thoughts and words that needed to be said in a raw and candid way, to try and help other parents of children who have chosen to die, not feel quite so alone. It's also given me insight into what I need and want to heal if I am to enjoy a fuller and brighter life.

Thinking about peace and going back to my certainty I can find the inner stillness that I crave once the warring emotions within me end, I do hope that I'm right. As I've taken the time to pick through the pieces left of me and shared all I have with you throughout these pages, I've come to trust that knowing what I struggle with gives me something concrete to work on going forward in my healing. I truly do want to love you with more than just my pain.

If I knew then what I know now, I'd tell every bereaved parent looking for peace to expect it to be a long road. I still don't know for certain whether grief is made more difficult by our circumstances or we grieve the way we do, despite them. I only know that along the way, I've experienced more loss, relationship problems, financial difficulties, family conflict, and health challenges: all major areas of life that when negatively impacted, challenge us to achieve anything more than what we need for our immediate survival.

It is essential that anyone trying to heal feels safe in their living and work environment. In my view, it is impossible to heal against a backdrop of anything that feels threatening. But to maintain balance and find peace, anyone suffering needs to understand the pain they're in and know how to tend to it throughout their grief. This will require searching for information and resources, finding the right type of support and acquiring the skills and tools along the way to help them survive the challenging times and feel successful on the path of healing that is right for them.

No one gets through being a bereaved parent unscathed. However, everyone has different needs in grief. There will be plenty of ups and downs. It is essential that those new to grief learn how to deal with the triggers they soon will learn can attack relentlessly and set them back, even after all the gains they've made. These setbacks are temporary. More gains will be made.

In my current experience and no longer wanting to fight any battles, real or in my mind, pursuing peace for me is now about maintaining the stability I have created in my life. This includes health, relationships, family, finances and doing what feels fulfilling. None of which was possible to fully understand, never mind obtain in my earlier grief. There have been numerous obstacles, course corrections and actions that I've had to take that felt darn right scary. But I'm here. Still standing. Doing better. The same as every bereaved parent farther along this path than those of us coming up behind them.

I now recognize that it can feel better to hold on to pain that is familiar. It feels comforting, even if this can only be in less than healthy ways. Which I'd suggest is a major factor impeding anyone's ability to fully heal.

For years I thought I could find peace by accepting how life had turned out for me as a mom and for our family. Drawing largely on my belief that all things happen in their perfect time and order, I thought acceptance was the major piece missing from the healing puzzle. Once I understood more about trauma and the symptoms of PTSD that can be or are a very real part of grief related to child loss and impedes our healing, I let go of my expectations for what my healing should look like. I am letting the journey unfold. Curious about where it's taking me.

It is imperative that grieving parents understand that they can only be responsible for their healing. It gets complicated when surrounded by loved ones who have not achieved the same results or are not meeting someone else's expectations. To get through any conflict and misunderstanding that is most likely to occur between partners, immediate and extended family members, honest communication about what loved ones can and cannot tolerate from each other, while still feeling compassion for what the other person is experiencing, can reduce much of the tension.

Today, I am happy to say I can smile more when looking at photos of my daughter and revisiting the handful of memories I sometimes do. I've put a stop to the harshest of the self-blame and anger I once felt, and am diligently working towards having fewer regrets and feeling less disappointment about how things turned out for us.

I would offer as a gentle reminder to others on this path that it takes time and patience to work through pain. It's natural after losing a child to think that some of it will always remain. To fully accept loss that is traumatic may not be possible for everyone. It is essential to remember that healing is not a race. It doesn't have to meet anyone's expectations; some that may not even be possible to meet. For parents trying to heal amidst a number of various pressures, it can be comforting to remember that trying to find peace and healing sometimes must be put on hold while they must concentrate on taking care of other things. Not to worry. Both will be waiting for them to find, one day.

Relief

I f it's not quite possible to attain peace, my darling girl, then it's important to talk about relief. I didn't learn the importance of relief until I was years into my grief. I'd been so focused on the end result of healing (preferring to skip past all the pain), I'd never stopped to think about what I needed to get there. Understanding all the ways that we can benefit by bringing relief into our healing changed my life. I shifted to a focused and more intentional approach by making decisions based on what would bring me the greatest amount of relief, regardless of what I might have to do. At that time, this meant leaving my job, downsizing and moving across the country.

Someone said to me at the beginning of these life changes I was about to make "see you on the other side". I didn't get it then, but now I do. This adage describes the wild trip I had to willingly take through a crazy period of time without any certainty of how I'd come out the other side. But I did know when I reached it. Which I felt as the calm and balance I'd been seeking, along with the freedom to pursue what I now do.

Thought about more generally, "the other side" is the beginning of a major journey we set for ourselves and all that we must conquer on our way to reaching a desired outcome. While I do believe that timing plays a crucial role before certain things can materialize in our lives (and there's usually a lot to learn until then), making decisions and taking action that brings us relief makes this journey easier.

Relief feels like we have this beautiful sense of lightness to our being, where all the stress and anxiety of whatever we are afraid of or worrying about disappears. Mentally and emotionally, it feels like a weight has been lifted from our shoulders as we allow ourselves to surrender to the moment.

Personally, and critical to any balance I must maintain in my life is being able to manage the anxiety I live with that is symptomatic of my Post-Traumatic Stress. I've found that any relief I enjoy comes from how quickly I can change my thoughts that are emotionally debilitating to ones that are logical and do produce solutions.

With our intelligence and with practice, everyone has the ability to balance themselves. Having said this, it is important that for those who suffer anxiety and those trying to support them that they understand changing debilitating thought patterns isn't easy. I've been working at this for years. When we are in a fit of anxiety, remaining calm and trying to convince ourselves we can fix what is rocking us to our core is hard!

Anxiety can be mentally and emotionally crippling. It can be physically harmful, too. We can freeze, become ill, lash out at those around us and take reckless action. Relief helps us let go of the debilitating fear that some catastrophe is sure to be the end result of whatever we are worrying about. Which, when surviving trauma and in complicated grief can be anything and everything.

Because I lived like this for years after you died, sweet girl, when I started to live more intentionally to find relief, first and foremost I decided to change my thinking and trust that all change was possible. That everything would turn out for the best. That I could and would get all the support and resources that I needed. Changing my thinking to a consistently more positive framework gave me the courage to take any action needed that would free me from all mental and emotional stress. Which, for the most part has been centered on bringing the balance into my life I now enjoy.

Rather than panic or react to people or situations, I focused on what was happening within and around me and what I needed to soothe myself whenever I felt triggered. The level of relief I felt was my best clue to whether I was "okay" or something needed to change.

Whether relief is felt temporarily or is long-lasting, it is the result of a change we've made that feels better and is healthier for us. We can't heal without making changes.

If I were to revisit my decisions that represent a turning point in my life after losing you, precious daughter, many of them in the first dozen years or so were impulsive or a reaction to some difficulty I was experiencing. While many of them brought valuable change to my life despite not ending my inner struggle, I think I did a decent job finding my way through the worst of my grief, though I wouldn't make some of those same decisions today.

While it is often said that grief is different for everyone, I disagree. I think it's what we experience in grief in our situations and relationships that is different, not the pain itself. I doubt there is one bereaved parent that can teach any other bereaved parent more about suffering the loss of their child than what all of us already know. In fact, there is a certain comradery I feel with every bereaved parent I meet. I'm sure they feel the same. For me, it's a relief just to be with them.

What those of us farther along the path can maybe help other parents newer to the path with is how to avoid some of the pitfalls of early grief. One of these is to know the difference between reacting to our environment and situations only from the instinct to survive, which is common in early grief, versus making thoughtful changes from introspection and practical decision-making. Because it takes time to sort through all the chaos to find our way back to living, it's far more soothing and beneficial to focus on only deciding those things that can bring us immediate relief versus trying to solve all the problems at once.

Relief helps us develop an understanding of what we need as we rebuild our life. Anything that feels distressing in our environment or with our relationships is our mind and body's way of telling us what needs to change.

While we can't necessarily just stop being around negative people or meeting certain responsibilities, adjustments can be made in our life to reduce the stress. Knowing the type of environment, friends and activities we prefer; identifying what we need in our relationships to feel loved and supported; thinking about a different lifestyle that feels more comforting, gives us clues about how we can start to reimagine our life. Sometimes in ways we don't think are even possible.

Making choices based on what brings us the most relief sometimes is painful or means we must compromise. Giving up relationships that no longer feel mutually supportive or activities because they are too painful a reminder of what was, can happen. I still remember selling my piano. I felt enormous pain saying goodbye to yet another part of my past I could no longer identify with; but the relief I felt knowing it was going to a great family was enormous. I've experienced countless similar moments since, having to exchange what *was* for what *is* based solely on what has brought me the most relief.

Relief gives us respite from experiences that are unpleasant and feel distressing. It can arise from something that has ended or never happened at all. When we feel relief from something that's been avoided (like all the times I've felt relief knowing the family is safe) or when pressures have been alleviated (like when we finally sold the house and I was able to move back home to the ocean and the mountains), it feels freeing.

I prefer living with the feeling of freedom flowing through my body. It lessens much of the struggle I'd rather do without. I want others to feel this way too and as soon as possible in their grief. It took me far too long to get it.

If I knew then what I know now, I would tell newly bereaved parents to be mindful of the relief they feel, especially amidst the chaos, when they can. Having said this, I get that it can be hard to know what feels comforting because child loss is so traumatic and the grief debilitating. Also, newly bereaved parents often don't feel deserving of anything that feels soothing.

So, while the first few months or year of grief may not be the time they can pay heed to the inner warnings of their mind and body screaming out for help, when the initial chaos has subsided sufficiently, it is important that the newly grieving start conditioning their mind to choose more from intention than react in anger and frustration to what they feel they can't control. Some things to think about (or write a list) to help:

1.   What they can and want to do that would feel comforting.
2.   The type of environment that would feel more peaceful.
3.   What would be better to give up or avoid.
4.   What they need help with and whom they can count on to help.
5.   Whether all of their family's needs are being met and if not, what they need from their partner or someone else. *Have the courage to ask!*
6.   The state of their relationship and what needs to change.
7.   Their health and if they have sufficient support in place from their employer, insurance company and/or other

financial institutions to get them through any potential work adjustments, job loss or other difficulties that may arise.

While it may seem like the above exercise would require too much effort, this list represents only some of the challenges that can cause bereaved parents and their family serious setbacks in grief. Grieving parents find they cannot work, must change jobs or career, get sick and argue. Surviving children get sick too and face many other difficulties in their grief. Maintaining their school and social life absolutely requires help, which may not always be easy to find. It's imperative that parents try to put a support system in place as soon as possible for surviving children. They can let teachers and other adults active in their child's life know there's been a sibling death in the family, to watch for any signs of trouble and alert the parents.

Reacting to problems is often the only way newly bereaved parents can cope. They don't yet have the skills and objectivity to assess what they need and want. However, with time comes awareness and the understanding that most people are willing to help when asked. Grieving parents must know what they need and have the confidence to ask for help when it becomes apparent no one is coming to rescue them.

I would tell parents who are newly bereaved to always remember that they are not and never will be alone in their grief and struggle. There are others going through what they are. If they are lucky, they will have family and hopefully a good friend or two by their side to help and comfort them. There are online support groups and maybe one in the area they live they can attend in person for a personal connection and help.

By knowing what they need in grief, not only will grieving parents be able to take better care of themselves, which is an essential part of healing, but they can guide loved ones to make choices to improve their lives too. Change occurs over time. Setting their sights on what they need and want now or in the future can ensure these changes actually happen, but the key is knowing when and how to take action that is needed.

I am a firm believer that everything happens when it's supposed to. Change requires patience. I knew five years before we sold our home that we would have to move. It took another two years before we settled down in our new location. These in between times waiting for change can feel distressing. We all need relief from the stress and worry.

I would suggest to anyone feeling distressed to remain calm. Decide whether their needs have been met for today. If yes, leave worrying about things until tomorrow, when a fresher mind will prevail, and new ideas can materialize. Brainstorm solutions with a partner and children where age appropriate and decide together what can be done to tackle the immediate problem.

Finally, it is good to remember that even on the worst days, life always looks a little better after rest and quiet contemplation.

Intention

I have a lot to say about intention, darling girl, but I'll start with the obvious. Which is to reassure you that I did have good intentions raising you. I did intend with every choice I made that we would remain one tight and happy family, even if I did seem a little overzealous about some things. Everything went sideways after you died. I've struggled since to find the error of my ways.

The few people who know about my struggle with this issue have assured me I did the best I could with what I knew at the time. (You told me yourself I was a great mom, just before you died.) That my efforts to ensure the success of our family were normal for anyone wanting the same for theirs. Perhaps they were right. Maybe I am being harder on myself than I should be. That it's time I start easing up on all the self-criticism.

I started out the same as all new parents who have the intention to love and protect their children throughout their life, no matter what. That we think about you as extensions of ourselves is never made clearer until you are gone. And when this happens; when you die, the first thing that we do as grieving parents is question where *we* went wrong. It's often never about you.

It seems in general that as parents, we can't separate entirely the individuality of our children from ourselves or see the truth of who you really are when things start to go awry. This is evident by the fact we only ever boast about your accomplishments when things are going well, but never when there are problems and things aren't going very well.

When things do go off the rails and when you are no longer here, it's easy to take on all the blame and feel like the failure it seems we are at being good and decent parents. For not having known more and done better to protect you. This too, is made clear by how silent we become immediately after you are gone. How hesitant we are to talk about you in our grief, if we ever get the chance.

As a parent with good intentions from the start, I honestly never planned for anything to go wrong. Not for you or anyone else in the family. What parent does? Since you died, my darling girl, I've found that no parent plans for dealing with crises or the death of their child. It's not something we are wired to do. We want and hope for things to always be okay.

So, when a death does occur suddenly and unexpectedly, the blame for such catastrophe naturally falls squarely on the shoulders of those who feel the most responsible. We the parents, who felt so certain that the vision we had for our family based on all our efforts and good intentions, would be how life would actually go. It's been really hard for me to accept that this is *not* what happened.

I've struggled for years trying to understand *you literally choosing to die*. It's not how I raised you to think or be or what I thought we had in terms of closeness, truth and trust. I trusted you would talk to me about anything troubling you (I think planning your death qualifies). It's been almost as painful knowing how wrong I was about all this as it's been to physically lose you. I can't tell you how many times I've stared at one or another of your photos, dumbfounded. Still unable to truly understand when and why it all went so wrong.

I've said for years that it's so difficult for parents, or anyone trying to support someone vulnerable, to know their true pain and misery. I've been told by therapists and medical doctors that not even they can ever really know the intentions of anyone at risk of suicide. And this is just treating those who do seek help. Many don't. As hard as this is to write, I think it's the truth. Which means how could I or anyone else close to you have really known your intentions?

Considering this as a reality does alleviate some of the pressure that I've long felt believing I should have known better. I should have done more. I should have been able to see that something was critically wrong; way beyond the things I worried about in general. But, I didn't.

Mental health let alone suicide wasn't talked about openly fifteen years ago. Even today we have a long way to go to discuss suicide more openly. In the context of this environment, my focus was on helping you thrive and get the most out of life (you were so smart and beautiful). I believed you could have it all. I wanted you to believe this too. The reality is that not everyone wants to experience the world this way. You, my girl, were one of them. Which, I think you tried to tell me.

Regardless of all I taught you about going after what you wanted and supporting you in every way, I couldn't see, never mind accept that none of this really mattered to you. Clearly, my intentions for you weren't the same as those you had for yourself. That I didn't see this and couldn't help you more still feels so painful.

It wasn't until after you were gone, and I inherited all the angst you must have felt when you were here that I understood what you must have been going through. While the cause and reasons for our suffering were different, the pain we felt I'm sure was similar. It's a pain I understand that only we can fix. And many people don't know how.

Before your death, I had been driven by a model of success that hinged on me having an intention and going after what I wanted.

Best-case scenario was to let things fall into my lap. Which they often did. I thought I was setting a good example for you about how easy life can be when we trust in our own and some higher power. And while the better part of me still believes this (the part that keeps me pushing to pursue all that I do), I can't deny how difficult it's been to trust in life the way I did.

I've thought a lot about intention moving forward in my life. It's been difficult to think too much about what I want, when what I know I really do, I simply can't have. That would be *you* and life the way it was before. Even if this meant giving up everything I've gained since you've been gone. Knowledge, experience, finding my purpose. I'd give all these up in a second just to have you back.

I'd imagine this is the reason why I've been hesitant to think too much about my future. While I love and am committed to the work I do, the zest I feel for life fluctuates. Ideas I get. But not knowing whether I'll have the health, energy and interest to keep things going stops me from pursuing life with gusto. Which is such a change from how I used to be.

If I knew then what I know now, I'd tell newly bereaved parents or those struggling in grief that intention does eventually become important to one's healing. While it is directly linked to a manifestation practice and usually is thought of as pursuing material things (and there is loads of information available on that topic online), related to complicated grief intention has a different meaning.

Just trying to survive early grief, it can be critical for bereaved parents to have the intention to have good health. To feel loved and supported in their relationships. To avoid financial difficulties. To find the help they need. To not suffer anymore. To find passion and a purpose to help them make sense of their tragedy (many bereaved parents do something in the name of their deceased child). To have the strength and courage to carry on. To love and forgive themselves.

A couple of years after my daughter died, I took an intention and manifestation course and participated in several webinars on the topic to try to find some focus in my grief. None of the information was new to me, but my approach to life had changed significantly. I was looking for something I may be missing to help me create a better life amidst my suffering. While I valued the information presented, none of the approaches were geared toward what people who are suffering, need. The entire focus was on material gain.

Intention is powerful. People intend outcomes for their life every single day. But when we are suffering, what we need changes. Most people in pain aren't interested in collecting more material stuff and money is meaningless when it won't bring back our child. Which is why I had to rethink intention, and how it could be used for people trying to rebuild their life from tragedy and without much motivation because they are suffering.

Intention works. I know and have experienced throughout all my adult life that with the right amount of desire, we can create anything. But we must know what we want and believe that we can have in order to consistently enjoy the outcomes that we want.

Since my daughter died, I've spent years contemplating what would really make me feel complete. I am different now than from before. Because I still don't know what would make me feel fulfilled, I haven't been intending big things for my life. I've used intention just to bring me outcomes to relieve me from the pressures that I've felt. But it's different (and more fun) intending results just because we want them. Perhaps it's time I kickstart my intention practice into full swing again by being more focused on having fun.

I can say that sitting around waiting for things in life to get better won't produce concrete results. In this regard, I've always set goals I thought I could attain and would bring some structure to my life that feels stabilizing. At the same time, grieving parents must listen to their bodies and know when to modify or toss goals altogether. There is no such thing as quitting in grief. Only trying different things.

I really believe that we do in life what we are meant to do and in the timing that is right. Of course, we can opt out of doing whatever is compelling us to move forward. However, when we do choose to take on any role, we must be mindful that as bereaved parents, most of us aren't who we were. Pushing ourselves to do this or that may not hold the same interest. Our values and motivation may have changed. We may not have the energy or health to pursue goals like we once did.

In grief, using intention is a wonderful way to create an easier and healthier life. With good health, anything else we want is sugar on top. In early grief, bereaved parents can use it to create the smallest things to help them alleviate some of the horrendous suffering. To begin with, this may be sufficient time, space and quiet to rest. The courage to deal with whatever comes their way. Solutions to problems and opportunities to move them forward (this is especially important if they've changed so much, they don't know what they can do anymore). Eventually, intention can be used to fulfill desires they may envision for themselves and loved ones that are material or just for fun. They may also hold on to one or two throughout their entire grief that guide their healing. Such as they will *not* suffer. They *will* heal.

For example, right at the start of my bereavement, though I didn't see it as intention back then, I set a lifelong one to *never* allow myself to get stuck in pain. That I *would* find a way to heal (an intention I hold to this day). Beyond this and in the first weeks and months of my grief, I could only set the smallest of intentions each day. Initially, this was to get out of bed and see my then thirteen-year-old son off to school with a smile on my face. I wanted him to know that I was there for him, even if it didn't seem that way. Eventually, I intended to reduce my stress and eliminate all conflict that had arisen in my relationships. To let go of anger and center my thoughts in ones that were more positive. To have the courage to do whatever I needed to keep moving forward, one step at a time.

From there, and because I was adamant that I didn't want to waste one moment of my loss experience and to honor my daughter, I intended to always share what I learned with others. As this was a much bigger intention, and not really knowing what to do, I attended an Angelic Healing course in California. I was terrified of travel and trying anything new, but I forced myself to go. Following this, I set up a healing practice and wrote and published my first book *Divine Healing*, which took a few years. When it was time to go back into the world because I had to get a job, I focused my intentions on developing new skills, finding the right job and re-establishing my financial independence. All of which I did. The list goes on, though I'll recall here that most of what I intended throughout this period was to get me out of one situation to another in a way that brought me the greatest feeling of relief. Still, big or small, all of my intentions brought me the results I needed and wanted.

I would reassure the newly bereaved that they can intend more for their life once their basic needs have been met in grief. Otherwise, in my view it's still pretty much all about survival. While I recognize it's difficult to want much more than relief when they are suffering, it's important to remember that when they do start to overcome the worst of their pain, intending can be used for different outcomes. It can even be fun. For example, intending that perfect holiday they've always wanted to go on but thought they couldn't afford. It's feels great when it actually happens!

I would tell the newly bereaved to think of intention as nothing more than a mindful practice they can use to bring something that they need or want into their lives when it is the right time (sometimes this is immediately). When what they need and want is real, which means it will solve a problem or is a desire that comes from their heart, and they believe they can have it, they will create whatever they are intending.

I would encourage newly bereaved parents to trust that one day they will be able to create the life they can envision for themselves. While at first this may only be making a small change to their environment or manifesting something else to help them survive early grief (for me, it was someone to take my son so my husband and I could attend an evening support group once a month), intention used even in the smallest way after loss is one thing they *can* hold on to while everything else around them seems like it's crumbling.

Examples of intention statements:

I intend to end my suffering.
I intend to heal.
I intend to find the courage to meet all of my challenges.
I intend to find my right and perfect job.
I intend to end any existing conflict in all of my relationships.

For information related to intention, please see "Intention and Manifestation" under Resources at the back of this book.

Self-Worth

It is important to talk about self-worth immediately after intention; for without it, what would there be worth pursuing in life, darling girl? Self-worth is something millions of people struggle with. Just look at the loads of courses and retreats available to teach people how worthy they really are.

Why we come here only to struggle to love, respect and believe in ourselves, I have no idea. But I have found that it is these three qualities we must embrace if we are to live our best life. How much we love, respect and believe in ourselves influences what we want to do, trust we can do and will actually accomplish in our lifetime. All of which can change as we become aware of what we lack in these qualities and choose to overcome whatever is challenging us.

Self-worth is about having a good sense of our value as an individual. When we value ourselves, we respect what we are capable of and have contributed to our family and the communities we engage in. We feel confident we will accomplish whatever we are striving to do and get what we want because we trust in our ability to create outcomes in line with what we are envisioning. We are excited by life. Self-worth feels inwardly powerful, which is a beautiful feeling to have.

It makes me smile just thinking about all this because one, I know it's true; and two, just reminding myself of what life can be like again feels thrilling. It makes me want to jump right back in the game. However, because losing you, sweet girl, quite literally knocked me off my feet, it's been difficult to find value in all I do. Deep down, I believe I have failed spectacularly at the most important job I've ever had. That is, being your mom. And I'm not so certain how much we can actually love and value ourselves when we believe we are a failure in any area of our life. Obviously, we cannot think of ourselves as having failed.

It's only after taking time to reflect on the harm I've done to myself from enduring years of the grueling self-punishment that I've been able to see how little I really have loved, respected, valued and believed in myself since you died. I am now assessing what I need to do to repair all the damage. And while I do not wish to bemoan my perceived failures and inadequacies, they are important to acknowledge if I am to overcome them.

After losing a child and in our grief, it is natural to lose one's sense of self as we become consumed thinking about the error of our ways. All the obsessing makes it hard to respect and appreciate who we were and all we did to contribute to our family and communities and could again.

While I can accept we all have something good to offer, because we are judged more by what we do than who we are and it can take years to recover from the setbacks in grief that make it feel like we've been knocked out of the game, it can be hard to regain any sense of our abilities. Never mind any sense of our true worth to others.

As humans, we are wired to achieve. To succeed, we must feel confident in what we can do and that we will be valued as contributing members of society. Yet, for anyone else to see the value of what we can offer, we first must see this in ourselves. Probably the saddest part of grief is that it robs us of our ability to appreciate all that we can still bring to others, despite or even because of our suffering.

I can still recall the second I learned of your death, beautiful girl, and my world crumbling. I clearly remember the physical sensation. It was as though the life energy was draining right out of me. As time slowly passed and I felt like I was drowning in a sea of nothingness, it wasn't possible for me to grab hold of anything that made sense, much less believe I'd done anything right and everything had happened in its right and proper order.

These pages are filled with all I've tried to understand about your death and any role I may have played in your choice to die. Thinking about my worthiness within this context has not produced anything much of value.

The important thing right now is that I know I don't want to continue punishing myself for who I was or obsess about the past and things I may have done wrong. At some point, I realize I'll have to accept I did my best and whatever I did do wrong was *not* the deciding factor in your suicide. At least, I hope I'm right about this.

I'm not sure that whether you had left us an explanation for why you died, this would have helped me heal quicker from at least some of the pain from losing you. But, you didn't. We've all been left guessing, which has not helped anyone else who loved you resolve their pain, either.

I think all of this not knowing has kept me stuck in grief and the reason why I'm baring my soul to you. It's helped me sort through all that I'm still feeling and the suffering I want to free myself from that's gone on far too long.

If I knew then what I know now, I'd tell newly bereaved parents that grief is messy and isn't something that just goes away over time. They will beat themselves up and hold themselves down in their questioning and obsessing about everything. They will feel anger, shame, fear, failure, disappointment, regret. They will lose their dreams and hopes and have a longing for their lost child that is so painful, it can actually feel worse than the physical loss itself. They will be challenged to love, forgive, accept, respect, value and believe in themselves, and grieve as hard for who they were and all they had; feeling more uncertain than ever of who they now are and who they can become.

I wish I could tell newly bereaved parents that the grief will be easy to overcome, but I can't. It takes hard work and commitment to become the person they want to be after losing their child. But it can be done, even when the journey is long and so unforgiving. In fact, it may be that because it is our toughest experiences that present us with the greatest opportunities for growth and healing, how they achieve their transformation will become the focal point of their journey, rather than the grief itself.

A major part of healing is being able to feel self-worth, and to love and respect who they are, regardless of their mistakes. In grief, this will give to them a sense of what they can dream about again, believe they deserve and pursue in their own way and time, bearing in mind there isn't any rush. Not having these qualities can significantly set them back the longer they stay suffering.

I would reassure newly bereaved parents that one day, they *will* feel stronger. They *will* start to feel different from who they are today. They *will* go on living with more confidence and hope. Yet, it's worth remembering that some pain may run so deep that no amount of comfort, success or evolving into who they envision themselves becoming will be the guarantee that they can fully heal the pain from losing their child.

Like a river with its current, their loss experience may take them places they don't want to go. It may challenge them to appreciate life. Love like there's no tomorrow. Find peace. Soar with ambition. Feel a desire to want more. That's okay. The day any grieving parent can feel anything more than just their pain is a huge achievement all its own.

As they learn to live again, there is enormous value that comes with every bereaved parent knowing how they want to be treated in their grief and healing. Not only by others, but in the love, care and gentleness they can demonstrate for themselves to create a lasting foundation of self-worth that everyone needs to be their best.

Strength

I have often been told how strong I am. Years ago, before you died, precious girl, most of my friends leaned on me. I was fine with that. I didn't feel the need to lean on others. Somehow, I always found my way through every challenge quickly and with ease. This was even the case having you on my own and in a little town that had never seen the likes of you. People came to the hospital nursery window just to have a peak at this new girl in town (my room was right next door). I could hear them exclaim how beautiful you were and smile to myself. I was so proud of you already, despite not having a clue how I was ever going to master becoming a good mom or what our lives together would be like.

Your grandma was there too, of course. And friends came to visit throughout my week-long stay under my doctor's watchful eye. Partly, I'm sure this was to allow me to rest while settling into being a new mom. Partly, I'm sure it was because the hospital wasn't very busy (there was only you and a baby boy in the nursery). It was the early 1980s, when new moms could still enjoy an extended hospital stay.

Never in my wildest dreams could I have imagined, while cradling you and staring into your big brown eyes, that one day I would be forever mourning your death at only twenty-two years old. I was completely unaware of how little time I'd actually get to be with you.

I can't tell you how often I've thought about what it must be like for parents who have to face a countdown to the ending of their child's life. In some ways and as much as I hate to admit it, the suddenness of your passing was perhaps a blessing. We never saw it coming. We didn't have to deal with the dread of preparing for it. On the flip side, I'm not sure any of us affected by your death understand to this day, the full impact of the shock and trauma we were hit with. It all happened so fast. In a blur, really.

I'd never have guessed in a million years that the day before your death would be the last time that I'd ever see you alive. Or, the next morning when we spoke would be your final day on earth. The last time I'd get to hear your voice. A voice I've been so afraid I'd forget over the years (it's true you don't). Strange though, that I can only remember a few words you used to call out in that beautiful sing song voice you had, along with your little laugh.

I remember reading in a book right after you died (written by a bereaved parent) that you never forget your child's voice. Apparently, a lot of newly bereaved parents worry about this. While this felt somewhat reassuring then, today I wonder if these same few words and laugh I can still hear, but that continue to fill me with so much angst are doing me more harm than good. Deep down, I realize it is a gift to have this memory, but there is a definite pain I feel realizing I can never again hear any words beyond these few or learn anything more about you.

Thinking about this part of my grief, I am filled with sadness about what could have been. I constantly wonder what you would look like now. What you would be doing. How our family would have been different if you had lived. I remember how much I depended on your insight and wisdom and wish that I still could. How I miss you!

Never once after you died, did I underestimate the wisdom of your brother as he was growing up or now, or of our youth in general. I consider all young people capable of teaching their parents and other adults in their lives, many things; when we listen. We need to listen more.

So, what does all this have to do with strength? Everything. It takes a heap of mental and physical strength to survive against the odds. To continually find the courage to resist taking an easier road. To hold onto our faith or some belief as it's the only thing driving us.

It takes strength to know when to put our pain aside to help someone else in theirs. To show up when we don't want to. To compromise or give in. To not feel self-pity or blame others for our predicament.

It takes strength to not use excuses or avoid taking responsibility. To show our vulnerability. To make room in our heart for others. To admit when we were wrong and choose to make things right.

It takes enormous strength to be a parent of a child who dies; especially by their own hand. To rise up against the stigma and judgment, all while ardently protecting our child's memory. To honor them for who they were despite their grievous actions. To forgive ourselves our own wrongdoings. To be willing to love and respect ourselves again.

It takes strength to want to heal from our suffering so that we can love our lost child with more than just our pain. It takes even more strength to stay the course.

In the beginning of my grief, I didn't think I would ever find the strength to carry on. Everywhere I turned there were challenges. More than anything I wanted to be with you, my precious daughter. But I found a reason to live. I wanted to be here for your brother. Why I want to be here for myself has taken longer to figure out.

Over the years, while it seems I have focused more on my weaknesses than the strength it's taken to get where I am today, I can appreciate that none of my efforts have been in vain. I've never wanted to waste any of the important lessons in this loss experience. Having said this, it's been a daily grind trying to keep up with all that I've expected of myself.

It isn't until more recently that I've been able to carve out the time and space to undergo a greater scrutiny of where I'm at, years after losing you. Reviewing all that I have been through, I know for certain I don't want to live in pain forever. At some point, if I am to end all of my suffering to get more out of this life, I must be willing to adopt a much softer approach in how I view myself and this experience.

If I knew then what I know now, I would tell newly bereaved parents not to underestimate the strength they already have in grief. Whether or not they know it yet, it takes incredible strength just to walk away from hearing they have lost their child. It's a moment I'm certain no bereaved parent ever forgets.

Time gives all of us perspective. I've had years to look back at all the ups and downs and bad and good in my grief. In thinking about what I'd have wanted to know about strength at the very beginning of my bereavement, it would be that I could trust I'd always have the strength to find my way through all the pain and challenges, even in the worst of times.

Strength is born from making a decision to end whatever is troubling us. And as the saying goes: where there is the will there is a way. I have found this to be true.

I'd tell newly bereaved parents and those doubting their resolve to carry on, to not sell themselves short about how strong they really are, whether or not they can see this now. It takes strength and willpower to get on with life after losing a child and keep those they love going strong, too. They may be surprised at how often they will be seen as a source of strength and even inspiration to family, friends and people they don't even know who've heard about their story. It can be comforting to remember this.

I'd tell them that while they can trust they will get stronger over time, their strength can and likely will diminish here and there through the years. They may often feel wiped out from all the effort grief will demand from them. For example, some bereaved parents feel driven early in grief to do something in their deceased child's name. Always, this is for a good cause and to help others. I found out the hard way and after several years that I couldn't sustain the energy I needed to keep up the frantic pace of all I wanted to accomplish to honor my daughter. At least, not in combination with the host of other obligations I had at the time. I ended up on a work disability, which forced me to think about and ultimately make the changes to my life that would bring me the balance I so desperately needed and wanted.

It's important grieving parents pursue passion work to honor their child that no doubt will require commitment and long hours. It may have to start as a sideline effort amidst other obligations. In all the busyness, they can benefit from remembering they only have to walk through their grief; not try to run or leap through it. Making decisions that bring them the greatest relief *at any moment* will help to create the overall balance they will always need.

While knowing precisely what they need and making "the better" choice to meet these needs all of the time isn't always possible, and every parent's situation is unique after child loss, grief is not. It can and does attack the mind, body and spirit. It ruins relationships, families, careers, health and the very foundation on which we have built our adult life.

While it may be preferrable for most of us to want to run and hide from our pain, it always catches up with us in some way. Amidst the confusion and challenges in grief, quiet and frequent reflection is useful to give bereaved parents a better sense of where they have been, where they are now and where they want to go with regard to their healing, relationships, family, health, lifestyle, career, job, personal growth, finding their passion and purpose in life.

Truly appreciating what they have already accomplished; how strong they are and what they are capable of takes time for all bereaved parents. It is through this process of quiet reflection that they can more accurately gauge the changes they need and want to make in their life and the time it may take to make them. It also provides a structure or framework for their healing.

Time is a mixed bag in grief. At first, it can feel like a life sentence of misery and pain. Eventually, it can give bereaved parents an appreciation for their life having deeper meaning than before. That healing sometimes happens in ways it couldn't have without certain painful experiences. That what they feel, do, believe, change or heal from doesn't have to be rushed.

I would urge newly bereaved parents to remember that while they may feel alone continuously having to battle all the unpleasantness that comes after losing a child, they're not. While their natural instinct may be to feel defensive in pain and isolate themselves, it's also good to remember that no matter where they are in grief, they sometimes must rely on the strength of others.

Initially and way past the initial two weeks to a month when many people may be coming and going from their life, it's helpful for bereaved parents to form a close circle of friends and family with whom they can share what they are feeling and trust to help with their immediate needs. These are people who can respect the family in grief, but still offer connection and support to give grieving parents that feeling of having a soft place to fall whenever weariness overcomes them, as it surely will. It also feels like a huge relief to have people around who aren't afraid to just be with them in their suffering. This helps to diminish some of the awkwardness, isolation and difference from everyone else that they immediately start to feel after losing their child.

In terms of support, bereaved parents may need help with babysitting or a ride for surviving children, or would appreciate one or two of their child's friends coming over to the house to hang out (they may be surprised how quiet a grieving household can be and how many adult friends back away). They may appreciate a home-cooked meal. Help with the laundry or light house cleaning. Someone to walk the dog or a visit with a friend. True friends are like nuggets of gold. They don't use the excuse that they didn't want to intrude on the newly bereaved or that they stayed away because they've been really busy.

Once the family does return to some routine, it's essential that bereaved parents find the courage to ask for help from the right people should (when) issues arise related to work, health, finances and children. Without knowing what all of this will be, the point is that all bereaved parents and their surviving children need ongoing support from people who can and may even have a responsibility to help them through their challenges.

It is imperative that everyone in the grieving family's life after child loss (extended family, friends, employer, doctor, therapist, educators, minister etc.) understand that all surviving loved ones need time and space to regain their strength and sense of self amidst the sudden changes. People who can or have a responsibility to provide support should do so in a way that benefits the grieving the most (this may require them to learn about grief). Having an understanding of and compassion for whatever the grieving individual is going through will not only be enlightening for them, but also, they can trust will bring incredible relief to the person they are assisting.

Completion

My dearest darling daughter, when I think about completion, I think about so many things. The many wants and wishes I've had for things to be different. Now and most definitely in the past. About your life and completion on this planet. What your death has meant for me (my life shattered) and everyone else impacted by it. About all I could have possibly done for you and because I didn't, what I now can do to truly accept losing you to find me, again.

I've also been thinking a lot about what it means to close a life chapter and whether this is required if I am to let go of all my grief (I'm not even sure this is possible). Or, whether I'd be better off just trying to tuck away my existing pain and go on living the best I can, despite it. But then, because I'm a firm believer that pain catches up with us anyway, this doesn't sound like the better way for me to go.

I wonder too, whether there ever really can be completion of any kind after losing a child. Whether I'm sounding more hopeful than realistic. This last is critically important to consider because it's the difference between me believing I can fully heal or not. Which is a highly personal question every grieving parent likely will consider at some point in their grief.

I do realize that what one can achieve in healing, another may never. And that's okay. There's no right or wrong. It's just that the isolation I often feel in my pain has made me question whether it's normal to struggle so much, or whether I should be doing more to get over losing you, my precious child.

I know from the pain still in my heart, and despite the enormous strides I have made, your death has affected me at such a deep level; it's as though it changed my DNA. I'm no longer the same. The recovery I've been looking for seems a long way off.

Your death is the one thing I can't seem to "get over". I've concluded I can only try to do my best and leave the rest to fate. Even if this is to never truly part from all my sorrow. While this last may sound rather dismal and not what anyone in pain (including me) really wants to contemplate for their future, it's not unrealistic to consider that lasting grief may be a reality for many, if not most, bereaved parents.

While there are many things to heal after losing a child: health, relationships, family, one's faith; healing a broken heart is an entirely different matter. And it is the broken heart I mostly think of whenever I speak about healing and completion. How can a broken heart truly be fixed? I've read it's an actual thing people die from. I'm sure your grandma did. I've often wondered why I haven't.

Closing a life chapter may seem the sensible thing to do to help anyone get over something terrible. It's also symbolic of a part of our life we have outgrown. We all let go of chapters. Yet, for me to even consider mentally closing that chapter of my life where I was your mom (I accept it's physically over), I'd have to no longer be in pain thinking about the past with you in it, or find value in longing for the relationship we once had. Neither of which are true. Even though, you're there. I'm here. We're not together anymore.

I admit, I still think of our relationship mostly as a mom and daughter one, in an ethereal sort of way. I've tried to let imagining us in this way go too, by thinking of your existence only as the eternal being you now are. Something I am not (at least not completely while in this body). Which makes our chance of physically meeting up again while I'm still here next to impossible, regardless of what I believe. Which also hurts to think about.

How can you possibly outgrow feeling like a parent to a child who is gone or not always feel sorrow because they *aren't* here anymore? To not wish for things to be different. To not long for you to be here?

Without doubt, losing you meant losing me. How I'm to recover from this is a question I've grappled with for years. I fluctuate between believing there *is* a way I can fully heal from the pain of our physical separation, to having no hope at all of figuring this one out.

As I sit and stare at your picture, I still must catch my breath and force away the lump of pain that arises in my throat. The ache, gnawing at my heart.

When I think about completion, I have a long way to go to experience anything that even comes close to resembling a life where I could feel there was nothing lacking. Where I could feel a completeness to my being. On the contrary, our family isn't complete without you. I don't even try to pretend it is. Your prolonged absence represents the one piece missing from a puzzle that without it, the picture never can be made whole.

Nor do I have all of the information that would allow me to fully understand your death and how I could end up feeling so betrayed by you. When did I become such an insignificant part of your life that you could ever imagine your death would not make me feel so lost? Was I not important enough for you to stick around? Did you not trust that together, we could get through anything? I never wasn't there for you. I'm just not sure you knew this or cared.

I have considered too, that by choosing only to embrace positive emotions, moving forward I could shape my life the way

I want. I could put an end to all my suffering related to this last extraordinarily painful chapter. That by being accepting, forgiving and grateful for all I have experienced, this would help me feel inspired and get excited about the future. One where I could enjoy a fuller, and emotionally richer life.

Yet, it seems impossible, I could just will myself to do this by only changing what I think and feel. I've tried. We are hardwired to react emotionally to change. After loss and trauma, it's easy to fall prey to negative emotions. It takes knowledge and skill to shift ourselves away from just trying to survive our painful experiences, to steering ourselves through life with intention. And there is no doubt this is my preferred way to live.

Our emotions shape how we experience every moment. While for everyone, emotions are fleeting, whether we typically respond or react to our life situations is based on the way our brain developed in utero, and childhood, from the experiences and circumstances to which we became accustomed. Because it may be that a predominant emotional state also emerged that influences how we heal, I've changed the way I now view healing, accounting for the added effort it may take to overcome our deep-rooted vulnerabilities.

Positive or negative, in general we learned to react or respond early in life to our situations dependent on whether we actually were and felt loved, nurtured and safe. If our experiences were overwhelmingly negative, the challenges we face in adulthood may be (and likely are) harder to overcome than if we had experienced a loving, happy and secure childhood.

As adults, the truth of what we believe and how we feel about ourselves and life is mirrored back to us by what we are mostly experiencing. Notwithstanding that personality does influence our emotions, generally speaking, happy and secure people respond to life with predominantly positive emotions. Their decisions are based on thought, logic and reasoning. Insecure and unhappy people are driven by predominantly negative emotions; many that are self-destructive. They feel disadvantaged by their circumstances and defensive. Their decisions are emotionally based, instinctual and reactionary.

Having said this, it's important to remember that no matter what type of background we come from, anyone can work hard as adults to overcome their vulnerabilities. And, when life is going smoothly, it's relatively easy to center ourselves in a more positive mindset. However, no matter how positive we were before our loss or how hard we've worked to overcome our earlier pain, all bereaved parents feel broken after losing their child. They all are at risk of being consumed by negative emotions; many that can be long-lasting.

It takes time to sort through the aftermath of child loss and even begin to have a chance at healing. However, it is possible that how and when we heal after losing our child, is dependent not only on how our brain developed, but on the predominant emotional state to which we were predisposed.

I've long believed a positive mindset can help anyone heal. But in and of itself, this is not enough. Thinking specifically about recovering from grief, while those who were predisposed to positivity early in life may struggle less in their efforts to heal, it's worth considering that the ultimate healing *anyone* can experience, no matter what their background was, may come down to their resilience and whether or not they view their loss experience as something to be overcome. Which is exactly what I've tried to do.

However, I also think it's true that trying to get back in the game of living after losing a child when we already feel vulnerable from earlier experiences, can feel disheartening, if not impossible. I can attest to how difficult it's been for me just to try and regain a sense of self and find my true place in the world again, my darling girl.

I think much of this angst comes from the trauma of your suicide. I learned that adult trauma can trigger childhood trauma, which plays havoc with our emotions and ability to think rationally. It can even cause us to acquire Post-Traumatic Stress Disorder (PTSD), which I'm sure is what happened to me. I have no doubt both have made my grief much more complicated than it otherwise may have been. But then, what bereaved parent wouldn't feel traumatized by the suicide of their child and experiencing complications in grief?

Not wishing to disparage my own (or anyone else's) childhood experiences, I admit to having worked hard to overcome them early in my adulthood, which helped me cultivate a positive mindset. That is, until your death. I've had to work just as hard since then not to let all the work I've done to appreciate this earth experience completely slip away. I think I owe both of us, more.

Our emotions and beliefs give us a window into how we can choose to think and feel differently when we don't like what we are experiencing. Our emotions are hard-wired. They can be understood and measured. Which is why maybe we can manipulate them by focusing our thoughts one way over another, which helps us change our beliefs. But our feelings are personal. They are the mental associations we have to our experiences that can produce a cycle of pain to last a lifetime when they linger. As they often do. For years. They are not so easy to influence.

It is critical to understand, that while positive thinking and learning how to steer our mind away from harmful thoughts does help with healing, the brain undergoes physiological changes after trauma and PTSD that affects the mind and body. We cannot heal from the trauma of child loss (or anything else) by only choosing to think positively. Bereaved parents experiencing trauma from losing their child or who may have unknowingly acquired PTSD, must learn what the symptoms are and how to manage those impacting them throughout their grief. They include irrational thoughts and volatile emotions (and there are many more) that can complicate grief early on.

Having learned much more about trauma in recent years and how to conscientiously manage my PTSD symptoms, I know there is power in being willing to look at things differently and focusing on thoughts that are opposite to those that undermine my healing. In fact, it is these two skills I rely on to keep going. There is completion too, in choosing to no longer have hope or faith, or the desire to move forward. Which is not the kind of completion I am looking for here.

What I do want is to be certain I haven't wasted a single moment not getting the lessons I am meant to from your death, my sweetest, precious daughter. That life for me can feel complete before it is my time to go. I'd hate to have to come back and do it all again.

Also, I really want to honor you as someone who was so much more than just another unfortunate young person who knew only suffering in her short life. You deserve to be recognized for all you did complete on earth, even though I certainly don't like the way it ended.

I like to think you experienced decades worth of living in the more than just two you did have here. That you had nothing more to finish when you left, even though it's natural for people to think you died way before your time. Which is not for anyone to judge, including me.

While I understand the death of every child and young adult can make people quick to assume you all left us way too soon, I have to consider that in wanting completion for myself (and maybe other bereaved parents feel this way too), maybe this isn't entirely true. We all have our own unique life path and manner in which we leave.

Certainly, from the spiritual beliefs I have, I understand that physical completion does not always occur in the time or way we would expect, or as the result of someone's long and well lived life coming to an end. While I believe we all must do whatever is in our power to try and save every soul; especially everyone at risk of suicide, for my own sanity, I must consider that maybe it's not always our role to do this.

Thinking this way alleviates some of the harshest self-criticism I've put up with for so many years; all because I believe I failed to do my part to save you, my beloved child. I have to consider now after suffering for so long, whether the greater plan for me has been to learn to let all the suffering go.

It's true, I've learned more from you and your passing than any living soul could teach me; as much as I hate to admit this (it's a love/hate thing). But, what you did, deep down I don't think was right or well-thought out. However, because I respect you far too much and will never do anything to tarnish all I have of you: which are my memories, I'd never condemn your choice to die.

In fact, I've never once waivered from my belief that your choice and the action that you took to end your life was between you and your maker, alone. That if it wasn't your time to go, you'd still be here.

I'm not sure what you believed about death and the beyond when you made that final call. I only know the police told me you were exceptionally beautiful in death and looked at peace when you were found. When we viewed your body a few days later at the funeral home, you did look like a sleeping angel.

Remembering this always brings me some peace whenever I do get caught up thinking about your final moments here on earth, which is still so hard to bear. Right from the beginning, I've felt blessed knowing that at least I'd never have to worry about what you may have seen.

What anyone believes about the possibility (or not) of our ongoing existence surely will determine what they experience in their grief. For years after you died, I worried about you being alone wherever you now are. That no one was there to meet you when you crossed over or hang out with you, whatever you are now doing. Strangely, I felt distressed by this.

Over time and after reading countless stories of people who survived near death and what many dying people, both young and old, claimed to have witnessed on their deathbed just before their passing, I feel reassured that our completion of this physical life is more a beginning of the next. One that is truly beautiful. Limitless. Freeing. A return to our true home. Thinking about your death this way is comforting and helps me feel less alone in our parting.

Completion means so many things. Not least, all that I would like to put away, including my wishes and wants. Regrets of the past. Any dreams I had for you and the family I still may be clinging to.

It's been awhile since I picked up a book on child loss, but I came across a couple of them recently. Both reminded me of the ongoing struggles all bereaved parents have trying to overcome their heartbreak from losing their child. One, published in 1997 and written by a psychologist, herself a bereaved mom, recounts the grief experience of dozens of bereaved parents who were at least five years into their grief. They shared the same stories of pain and struggle that all bereaved parents talk about, regardless of how much time has passed since they lost their child.

Reading their stories was like welcoming an old friend back into my life. Just as these bereaved parents said decades ago and years into their bereavement, I'd say to anyone new to child loss that life does go on. It may even and probably will get better after some time has passed, though I'd add, not without the effort required to make this happen. Combined, this is the courage, self-discipline, introspection, and commitment to healing based on their belief that there *can* be more to life than only suffering.

I don't know what completion will ultimately be for me, darling girl. Whether or not I finally will be able to let go of everything tying me to pain. What I do know is that for today, it's worth considering that healing may be more about me accepting my life, rather than struggling to accept your death. On the other hand, it still feels natural for me to think I'll always feel the death of you throughout my being until I am no longer here.

A contradiction of thought. But one that brings me both peace and pain. Peace, knowing I will have tried everything possible to make the most of my life without you in it. Pain, for the exact same reason.

If I knew then what I know now, I would tell newly bereaved parents that there is no easy road, maybe not even a certain destination when it comes to finding completion of any kind after losing their child. Whatever their journey will ultimately be, it's one everybody must take mostly on their own. It will be challenging, confusing and frustrating trying to keep up with their relationships (they can flip on a dime), family and various obligations.

My motto has always been: "Take care of yourself first and let your changes reflect on the loved ones around you." This is not selfish. In fact, it is essential to be aware of our own needs in grief if we are to heal and sometimes, lead others out of their pain. For parents in relationships, there's always going to be someone who is feeling stronger at any one time. It is beneficial to try and cultivate an environment where couples know that they can lean on each other for support.

For those with surviving children, it's a given that parenting them will not be what it was after losing a child. At least, for a time. However, tending to the needs of surviving children who are grieving too, must remain a primary focus for newly bereaved parents. It may be necessary to alter the care between partners. (I've written extensively about this in my book *Divine Healing Transforming Pain into Personal Power*.)

No bereaved parent should underestimate the considerable energy it takes to try to chart a course through grief without a compass. It's like trying to chop down a forest to create a path, not knowing where it will lead. Most people wouldn't willingly choose to do this. A bereaved parent is forced to.

Anyone who can find their way through all the different challenges that grief will throw at them, is the very definition of someone who has something worth sharing with others. I am certain that all bereaved parents appreciate a little guidance on their journey. I remain eternally grateful to all those who have shared their experience and knowledge, whether in person or books, to make my journey a little bit easier at times.

At some point, every newly bereaved parent will find that one day, they too are years into their bereavement. It can be comforting to remember that what they will accumulate in wisdom and experience can be invaluable to someone else starting out on their own path through grief. It can make the heartache and difficulties worthwhile.

There are so many firsts in grief related to child loss; it really can feel like we are being born again. Sometimes over and over. While this rebirth may be into a world that nobody wants to be in, here we are. With no way out. It is important that newly bereaved parents remember to take stock of their accomplishments, big or small throughout their grief. Little moments of significance add up and can help them gauge how they are healing. Like noticing the first time they can laugh again. See color in 3D. Feel a tiny spark of joy. Hum a little tune. All of these and more represent a completion of whatever immediately came before, no matter how small these first steps may seem to anyone else. They are HUGE for parents in grief.

Recently, I received an email from the adult sibling of my daughter's closest friend who died shortly after my daughter, from an illness. Her sibling and I hadn't corresponded for a few years, but it was like no time had passed at all. In thinking about my response, I discovered that this time apart was a wonderful opportunity to think back to all the good that had happened to both of us since we last communicated. And there was a lot of good and growth, despite the pain that still remained.

It is easy to become overwhelmed by the tragedy from child loss. However, allowing ourselves to get stuck in time robs us of our ability to appreciate how much we have grown and healed in our grief. Countless times throughout the years, I've needed reminders from my loved ones to help me appreciate how much I am doing and have already accomplished. Of all the good that surrounds me. Of all that's still ahead.

I want every bereaved parent to trust and remember that they too, will grow and heal, despite the pain. That they will have good in their life, again. That they do have a future, even if they can't see this yet. Surrounding themselves with family and friends who can help them celebrate the strength they have to survive, can be a big help.

It is also helpful that those impacted by the same loss of a beloved son or daughter, sister or brother, niece or nephew, grandchild, close friend or loving partner, feel compassion for each other. It is important to remember that they are all in the same boat, trying to survive their loved one's suicide. And, while what they will experience in grief will not be exactly the same, it won't be that different, either.

I would lovingly remind parents new to grief that after losing the most precious, irreplaceable gift of all – their child – to forgive themselves. To love themselves. To be kind to themselves. To trust that every step they take is leading them to the next part of their journey that is perhaps the toughest here on earth, for anyone to bear. It takes fortitude, insight and the belief that they can and will find their way to whatever destination awaits them.

For information related to child loss, please see "Child Loss" under Resources at the back of this book.

Resources

CHILD LOSS:
Bernstein, Judith R., Ph.D., *When the Bough Breaks: Forever After the Death of a Son or Daughter* ©1997,1998, 2011, Andrews McMeel Publishing LLC and Andrews McMeel Universal company, Kansas City, Missouri

COMPASSION:
https://www.compassionatemind.co.uk/
https://www.nicabm.com/blog/
https://self-compassion.org/

INTENTION AND MANIFESTATION:
Solis, Vonne, *Divine Healing Transforming Pain into Personal Power,* ©2011, 2018, Baico Publishing Inc., Ottawa, Canada and Gatekeeper Press, Columbus, Ohio
http://bit.ly/Living_Meditations

SHAME:
https://www.nicabm.com/blog/
Lee, Deborah A., DClinPsy and Sophie James, *The Compassionate-Mind Guide to Recovering from Trauma and PTSD: Using Compassion-Focused Therapy to Overcome Flashbacks, Shame, Guilt, and Fear* ©2011 New Harbinger Publications Inc. Oakland, CA.

SUICIDAL IDEATION:
https://www.verywellmind.com/suicidal-ideation-380609

SUICIDE STATISTICS:
CANADA
https://www.canada.ca/en/public-health/services/publications/
healthy-living/suicide-canada-infographic.html

USA
https://www.nimh.nih.gov/health/statistics/suicide.shtml

UK
https://www.samaritans.org/about-samaritans/research-policy/
suicide-facts-and-figures/

WORLD HEALTH ORGANIZATION (WHO)
https://www.who.int/mental_health/prevention/suicide/
suicideprevent/en/
http://apps.who.int/gho/data/node.main.MHSUICIDE
5YEARAGEGROUPS?lang=en

SUPPORT:
https://www.compassionatefriends.org/
http://tcfcanada.net/
www.goodgriever.com
http://bit.ly/Living_Meditations

TRAUMA:
https://www.nicabm.com/
https://besselvanderkolk.net/
https://www.ptsd.va.gov/professional/assessment/documents/
PCL-5_Standard.pdf
https://novopsych.com.au/wp-content/uploads/2020/04/pcl-5_
pdf.pdf

About the Author

Vonne Solís is the author of *Divine Healing – Transforming Pain into Personal Power, A Guide to Heal Pain from Child Loss, Suicide and Other Grief* (https://www.amazon.com/Divine-Healing-Transforming-Personal-Power-ebook/dp/B07K4TD6MG/) that offers thoughtful discourse on grief and loss in western culture, and a self-help therapy practice for individual transformation based on the powerful insights of angelic healing. Her second book *The Power of Change – A Path to Enlightenment* (https://books.apple.com/ca/book/the-power-of-change/id652998872) offers a 30-day guide to help others quickly start living a fuller, more intentional and joyous life.

After losing her twenty-two-year-old daughter to suicide in 2005, as an Angel Healing Practitioner and author Vonne has dedicated herself to healing and helping others to transform their life. Her latest book helps newly bereaved parents who have lost a child to suicide, to navigate early and complicated grief.

While the foundation for all of Vonne's work is based on the principles of self-responsibility and the choice we have to change, her experience with child loss, trauma and Post-Traumatic Stress Disorder, has given her a unique perspective and approach. She remains respectful of everyone's journey and the time and gentleness required for anyone choosing to recover.

For online support and resources and to connect with Vonne:

Blog: https://goodgriever.com/
Website: https://vonnesolis.com/
YouTube: http://bit.ly/Living_Meditations
LinkedIn: http://www.linkedin.com/in/vonnesolis
Facebook: fb.me/vonnesolisconsulting
Twitter: @VonneSolis

Made in the USA
Coppell, TX
06 June 2024

33180887R00154